GRANDMA'S BEST RECIPES

GRANDMA'S BEST RECIPES

HOME-MADE AND MUCH-LOVED favourites from GRANDMA's kitchen

First published in 2012
LOVE FOOD is an imprint of Parragon Books Ltd

Parragon
Queen Street House
4 Queen Street
Bath BA1 1HE, UK

www.parragon.com/lovefood

ISBN: 978-1-4454-9477-7

Printed in China

Introduction and Grandma's tips written by Linda Doeser
New recipes written by Beverly LeBlanc
Edited by Fiona Biggs
Additional photography and styling by Mike Cooper
Additional home economy by Lincoln Jefferson
Internal design by Sarah Knight

Notes for the Reader
This book uses both metric and imperial measurements. Follow the same units of measurement
throughout; do not mix metric and imperial. All spoon measurements are level: teaspoons are assumed
to be 5 ml, and tablespoons are assumed to be 15 ml. Unless otherwise stated, milk is assumed to be full
fat, eggs and individual vegetables are medium, and pepper is freshly ground black pepper.
For best results, use a meat thermometer when cooking meat and poultry – check the latest government
guidelines for current advice.
The times given are an approximate guide only. Preparation times differ according to the techniques used
by different people and the cooking times may also vary from those given. Optional ingredients, variations
or serving suggestions have not been included in the calculations.
Recipes using raw or very lightly cooked eggs should be avoided by infants, the elderly, pregnant women,
convalescents and anyone suffering from an illness. Pregnant and breastfeeding women are advised to
avoid eating peanuts and peanut products. Sufferers from nut allergies should be aware that some of the
ready-made ingredients used in the recipes in this book may contain nuts. Always check the packaging
before use.
Vegetarians should be aware that some of the ready-made ingredients used in the recipes in this book
may contain animal products. Always check the packaging before use.

Picture acknowledgements
The publisher would like to thank the following for permission to reproduce copyright material:
Vintage labels © AKaiser/Shutterstock
Close-up notepaper on cork board © Picsfive/Shutterstock
A coffee cup stain © Tyler Olson/Shutterstock
Masking tape © Samantha Grandy/Shutterstock
Vintage prints supplied courtesy of Istock Images

Contents

INTRODUCTION

When we are young children we love our grandmas unquestioningly, delighting in their undivided attention, their patient willingness to show us how to make cupcakes, the songs and rhymes they know and the stories of when they were little girls. Sadly, as we grow into adulthood and we become increasingly busy and preoccupied with our careers and children of our own, we can sometimes become a little bit dismissive of the older generation. But grandmas have a wealth of knowledge and experience to draw on – from preparing a celebration dinner so that everything is ready at the same time to tempting the appetite of a sick child with home-made soup, and from stocking the larder with a fabulous array of jams, jellies and preserves to providing nutritious and tasty family suppers all year round.

In fact, grandma is any family's greatest resource. Not only has she acquired knowledge and experience in numerous aspects of life, from raising a family to clearing a blocked drain, she is also the repository of family wisdom, having learned much from her own grandmother and mother. Moreover, people are living longer these days so many families are blessed not just with an active and vigorous grandma, but a pretty lively great-grandma too. Of course, not everything these matriarchs have learned over the years is appropriate to twenty-first-century life. Cleaning carpets by sprinkling them with damp tea leaves and later sweeping with a stiff broom is hardly fitting in the twenty-first century when tea comes in bags and everyone has a vacuum cleaner. However, much remains pertinent, whether it's how to manage a balanced family diet or a balanced family budget.

Today's grandmas are not little grey-haired old ladies, knitting in a fireside rocking chair. In their younger days, modern grandmas have witnessed great changes in the world and have been quick to take advantage of the best, most useful and most practical of them – whether buying non-iron fabrics or going late night shopping, making good use of the freezer or speeding up cooking in a microwave oven. Many of them had jobs outside the home and found ways to balance work and family life and most have had to cope with a few rough patches along the way.

Make the most of your matriarch

No one ever really learns from someone else's mistakes, but everyone can benefit from the things someone else got right. Not every grandma was a rocket scientist, but they have all acquired a vast amount of information and experience that has direct relevance to family life. When your little angel who always shared her toys and slept through the night suddenly turns into the ankle biter from hell who won't eat her greens and never takes turns on the swing, trust grandma when she says that nothing in childhood lasts and this too will change.

These days there are hundreds of thousands of books and probably millions of websites to turn to when you need the answer to a problem that is bothering you or you simply don't know how to do something. But how do you know that they are right? When grandma comes up with an answer, you know that she's been there and done that. Why does grandma make the best gravy in the world? Probably because she got it wrong a few times in the past but too long ago to bother about now.

(She scrapes up the sediment off the base of the roasting tin with a wooden spoon as the liquid cooks, adds a splash of wine to give it the richest flavour and keeps stirring.) Why is grandma's pastry so crisp and melt-in-the-mouth? (She rinses her hands under cold water and handles the dough as little as possible so that the fat – butter, always butter – doesn't melt.) Why are grandma's woollens so soft? (She reads and follows the washing instructions, even when it says hand wash!)

Most grandmas don't realize just how much they do know. They know practical things, such as how to whiz together a quick, tasty and nourishing snack in the blender with some fresh or frozen berries, a spoonful of honey and a carton of natural yogurt, useful facts, such as the ideal, safe temperature for a refrigerator is 4°C/40°F, clever tricks, such as adding two or three clean tennis balls to the tumble dryer when drying pillows or duvets to prevent the filling becoming lumpy, and time-saving tips, such as using kitchen scissors to chop herbs, anchovy fillets, ham, bacon, spring onions, sun-dried tomatoes and stoned olives.

From Grandma with love

Probably the very best thing about grandma is that she will do things for mum and dad and her grandchildren that she would never have the time, patience or inclination to do for anyone else in the world. Mum is often stressed and pushed for time, racing home after work, picking up the kids on the way and assembling the family meal before bath time and bedtime and then folding and ironing the washing. But grandma knows that a pre-schooler can spend a totally fascinated – and astonishingly quiet – half hour shelling fresh peas and, of course, will happily eat the fruits of his or her labour at supper. Grandma will always find time to do it – as well as making sandwiches stamped into moons and stars with biscuit cutters.

Grandma loves to share a weekend lunch or, better still, a celebration meal with the family and show off the culinary skills she has acquired during a lifetime of cooking – whether the menu is simple comfort food or classic family dinners. And any family in its right mind will relish these occasions too. The meal may not match up to the flamboyant and extravagant dishes of television's master chefs, but will invariably have been prepared with loving care and with a special eye on who likes what – only a grandma can do that. Grandma knows that people always appreciate food made with love, so take a leaf out of her book – whenever you're baking or making jams or preserves, make an extra batch or fill an extra jar, then package it up with style by cutting out and sticking on one of the labels

on pages 217–220. The labels can also be used as gift tags to add a personal and pretty touch, turning your home-made creations into a gift anyone would be happy to receive.

Grandmas passionately – maybe over-enthusiastically sometimes – want to pass on all the things they have learned in their long lives, whether first-hand or at their own grandmother's knee: a pinch of cayenne adds a delicious kick to a cheese sauce, cutting crosses in the stalks of Brussels sprouts is a pointless waste of time, halving vegetables and then slicing them flat side down prevents the knife slipping, cleaning the refrigerator with a solution of bicarbonate of soda avoids residual soapy smells, and it's okay to play some music and dance in the garden with the children late on a sunny Friday evening because they don't have to get up for school in the morning.

No – grandma doesn't know everything, although she knows a lot. What she hopes is that her daughters and daughters-in-law will value her wisdom and the wisdom of all the grandmas who have gone before and add to it as they reach that marvellous stage of life when they become grandmas themselves.

TRIED & TESTED FAVOURITES

Chicken Noodle Soup

SERVES 4–6
INGREDIENTS

- 2 skinless chicken breasts
- 1.2 litres/2 pints water or
  chicken stock
- 3 carrots, peeled and sliced
  into 5-mm/¼-inch slices
- 85 g/3 oz egg noodles
- salt and pepper
- fresh tarragon leaves,
  to garnish

1 Place the chicken breasts in a large saucepan over a medium heat, add the water and bring to a simmer. Cook for 25–30 minutes. Skim any foam from the surface if necessary. Remove the chicken from the stock and keep warm.

2 Continue to simmer the stock, add the carrots and noodles and cook for 4–5 minutes.

3 Thinly slice or shred the chicken breasts and place in warmed serving bowls.

4 Season the soup to taste with salt and pepper and pour over the chicken. Serve at once, garnished with the tarragon.

GRANDMA'S TIP
Clean hands are the fastest tools for shredding cooked chicken, flaking cooked fish, crumbling cheese and tearing delicate salad leaves and herbs.

Potato Pancakes

MAKES 12 PANCAKES

INGREDIENTS

- 4 large potatoes, peeled and coarsely grated
- 1 large onion, grated
- 2 eggs, lightly beaten
- 55 g/2 oz fine matzo meal
- 1 tsp salt
- pepper
- sunflower oil, for frying

TO SERVE

- soured cream
- thinly sliced smoked salmon
- snipped chives

1 Preheat the oven to 110°C/225°F/Gas Mark ¼ and line a heatproof plate with kitchen paper. Working in small batches, put the potatoes on a tea towel, fold over the tea towel and squeeze to extract as much water as possible.

2 Put the potatoes in a large bowl, add the onion, eggs, matzo meal and the salt. Add the pepper to taste and mix together.

3 Heat a large, heavy-based frying pan over a medium–high heat. Add a thin layer of oil and heat until hot.

4 Drop 2 tablespoons of the mixture into the pan and flatten slightly. Add as many more pancakes as will fit without overcrowding the pan. Fry for 2 minutes, or until crisp and golden underneath. Flip or turn with a palette knife and continue frying for a further 1–2 minutes, until crisp and golden.

5 Repeat this process using the remaining batter. Meanwhile, transfer the cooked pancakes to the prepared plate and keep warm in the preheated oven. Add extra oil to the pan between batches, if necessary.

6 Serve the pancakes hot, topped with soured cream and smoked salmon and sprinkled with chives.

IDEAL LIGHT BITE

Old-fashioned Chicken Stew

SERVES 6

INGREDIENTS

- 2 tbsp vegetable oil
- 1 x 1.8–2.25-kg/4–5-lb chicken, cut into quarters, backbone reserved
- 700 ml/1¼ pints chicken stock
- 700 ml/1¼ pints water
- 4 garlic cloves, peeled
- 1 bay leaf
- 4 fresh thyme sprigs
- 70 g/2½ oz butter
- 2 carrots, cut into 1-cm/½-inch lengths
- 2 celery sticks, cut into 1-cm/½-inch lengths
- 1 large onion, chopped
- 5 tbsp plain flour
- 1½ tsp salt
- pepper
- dash of Tabasco sauce

DUMPLINGS

- 200 g/7 oz plain flour
- 1 tsp salt
- 2 tsp baking powder
- ¼ tsp bicarbonate of soda
- 40 g/1½ oz butter, chilled
- 2 tbsp thinly sliced spring onions
- 60 ml/4 tbsp buttermilk
- 175 ml/6 fl oz milk

1 Put the oil into a large, heavy-based flameproof casserole, add the chicken pieces and cook over a high heat, turning frequently, for 10 minutes, until browned all over. Pour in the stock and water, add the garlic, bay leaf and thyme and bring to the boil.

2 Reduce the heat, cover and simmer for 30 minutes. Remove the casserole from the heat, then transfer the chicken to a bowl and leave to cool. Strain the cooking liquid into another bowl and skim off any fat that rises to the surface.

3 Put the butter, carrots, celery and onion into the casserole and cook over a medium heat, stirring frequently, for 5 minutes. Stir in the flour and cook, stirring constantly, for 2 minutes. Gradually whisk in the reserved cooking liquid, a ladleful at a time. Add the salt and some pepper and stir in the Tabasco sauce. Reduce the heat to low, cover and simmer for 30 minutes, until the vegetables are tender.

4 Skin the chicken pieces and remove the meat from the bones, tearing it into chunks. Stir the chunks into the cooked vegetables, cover the casserole and reduce the heat to the lowest possible setting.

5 To make the dumplings, sift the flour, salt, baking powder and bicarbonate of soda together into a bowl. Add the butter and cut in with a pastry blender or rub in with your fingertips until the mixture resembles coarse breadcrumbs. Add the spring onions, buttermilk and milk and stir with a fork into a thick dough.

6 Increase the heat under the casserole to medium and stir well. Shape the dumpling dough into large balls and add to the casserole. Cover and simmer for 15 minutes, until the dumplings are firm and cooked in the middle. Remove from the heat and serve immediately.

Steak & Kidney Pudding

SERVES 4

INGREDIENTS

- butter, for greasing
- 450 g/1 lb braising steak, trimmed and cut into 2.5-cm/1-inch pieces
- 2 lambs' kidneys, cored and cut into 2.5-cm/1-inch pieces
- 55 g/2 oz plain flour
- 1 onion, finely chopped
- 115 g/4 oz large field mushrooms, sliced (optional)
- 1 tbsp chopped fresh parsley
- 300 ml/10 fl oz (approx) beef stock, or a mixture of beer and water
- salt and pepper

SUET PASTRY

- 350 g/12 oz self-raising flour
- 175 g/6 oz suet
- 225 ml/8 fl oz cold water
- salt and pepper

1 Grease a 1.2-litre/2-pint pudding basin.

2 Put the prepared meat into a large polythene bag with the flour and salt and pepper and shake well until all the meat is well coated. Add the onion, mushrooms, if using, and the parsley and shake again.

3 For the suet pastry, mix the flour, suet and some salt and pepper together. Add enough cold water to make a soft dough.

4 Reserve a quarter of the dough and roll out the remainder to form a circle big enough to line the prepared pudding basin. Line the basin, making sure that there is a good 1 cm/½ inch hanging over the edge.

5 Place the meat mixture in the basin and pour in enough of the stock to cover the meat.

6 Roll out the reserved pastry to make a lid. Fold in the edges of the pastry, dampen them and place the lid on top. Seal firmly in place.

7 Cover with a piece of greaseproof paper, cover that with a piece of foil, pleated to allow for expansion during cooking, and seal well. Place in a steamer or large saucepan half-filled with boiling water. Simmer the pudding for 4–5 hours, topping up the water from time to time.

8 Remove the basin from the steamer and take off the coverings. Wrap a clean cloth around the basin and serve at the table.

GRANDMA'S TIP
Sharpen knives regularly, as blunt ones slip more easily and may cut you. Store in a knife block or on a magnetic rack out of the reach of children.

Shepherd's Pie

SERVES 6

INGREDIENTS

- 1 tbsp olive oil
- 2 onions, finely chopped
- 2 garlic cloves, finely chopped
- 675 g/1 lb 8 oz good-quality minced lamb
- 2 carrots, finely chopped
- 1 tbsp plain flour
- 225 ml/8 fl oz beef stock or chicken stock
- 125 ml/4 fl oz red wine
- Worcestershire sauce (optional)
- 1 quantity Perfect Mash (see page 118)
- salt and pepper

1 Preheat the oven to 180°C/350°F/Gas Mark 4.

2 Heat the oil in a large, flameproof casserole, add the onions and fry until softened, then add the garlic and stir well.

3 Increase the heat and add the meat. Cook quickly, stirring constantly, until the meat is browned all over. Add the carrots and season well with salt and pepper.

4 Stir in the flour and add the stock and wine. Stir well and heat until simmering and thickened.

5 Cover the casserole and cook in the preheated oven for about 1 hour. The lamb mixture should be quite thick but not dry. Season with salt and pepper to taste and add a little Worcestershire sauce, if using.

6 Spoon the lamb mixture into an ovenproof serving dish and spread or pipe the mash on top.

7 Increase the oven temperature to 200°C/400°F/Gas Mark 6, place the pie at the top of the oven and cook for 15–20 minutes until golden brown. Finish off under a medium grill until the topping is crisp and brown.

Toad in the Hole

SERVES 4

INGREDIENTS

- 115 g/4 oz plain flour
- pinch of salt
- 1 egg, beaten
- 300 ml/10 fl oz milk
- 450 g/1 lb good-quality
  pork sausages
- 1 tbsp vegetable oil, plus extra
  for greasing

1 Preheat the oven to 220°C/425°F/Gas Mark 7.

2 To make the batter, sift the flour and salt together into a mixing bowl. Make a well in the centre and add the egg and half the milk. Carefully stir the liquid into the flour until the mixture is smooth. Gradually beat in the remaining milk. Leave to stand for 30 minutes.

3 Grease a 20 × 25-cm/ 8 × 10-inch ovenproof dish or roasting tin.

4 Prick the sausages and place them in the dish. Sprinkle over the oil and cook the sausages in the oven for 10 minutes, until they are beginning to colour and the fat has started to run and is sizzling.

5 Remove from the oven and quickly pour the batter over the sausages. Return to the oven and cook for 35–45 minutes, until the batter is well risen and golden brown. Serve immediately.

Ham & Potato Pie

INGREDIENTS

- 225 g/8 oz waxy potatoes, cubed
- 2 tbsp butter
- 8 shallots, halved
- 225 g/8 oz smoked ham, cubed
- 2½ tbsp plain flour
- 300 ml/10 fl oz milk
- 2 tbsp wholegrain mustard
- 50 g/1¾ oz pineapple, cubed
- salt and pepper

PASTRY

- 225 g/8 oz plain flour, plus extra for dusting
- ½ tsp mustard powder
- pinch of salt
- pinch of cayenne pepper
- 150 g/5½ oz butter
- 125 g/4½ oz mature Cheddar cheese, grated
- 2 egg yolks
- 4–6 tsp iced water
- 1 egg, lightly beaten

1 Bring a saucepan of lightly salted water to the boil, add the potatoes, bring back to the boil and cook for 10 minutes. Drain the potatoes and set aside.

2 Meanwhile, melt the butter in a separate saucepan over a low heat. Add the shallots and cook, stirring frequently, for 3–4 minutes until beginning to brown.

3 Add the ham and cook, stirring, for 2–3 minutes. Stir in the flour and cook, stirring, for 1 minute. Gradually stir in the milk. Add the mustard and pineapple and bring to the boil, stirring. Season to taste with salt and pepper, then add the potatoes.

4 To make the pastry, sift the flour, mustard powder, salt and cayenne pepper together into a bowl. Add the butter and cut it into the flour, then rub in with your fingertips until the mixture resembles coarse breadcrumbs.

5 Stir in the cheese. Add the egg yolks and water and mix to a smooth dough, adding more water if necessary. Shape into a ball, cover and chill for 30 minutes.

6 Preheat the oven to 190°C/375°F/Gas Mark 5. Cut the pastry dough in half, roll out one half on a lightly floured work surface and use to line a large pie dish. Spoon the filling into the pie dish. Brush the edges with water. Roll out the remaining pastry and press it on top of the pie, sealing the edges. Make a small slit in the centre or use a pie funnel.

7 Decorate with the trimmings. Brush with the beaten egg and bake in the preheated oven for 40–45 minutes, until golden brown. Serve immediately.

GRANDMA'S TIP
Shallots and baby onions are easier to peel if you first soak them in hot water for 5 minutes and then drain.

Fisherman's Pie

SERVES 6

INGREDIENTS

- 900 g/2 lb white fish fillets, such as plaice, skinned
- 150 ml/5 fl oz dry white wine
- 1 tbsp chopped fresh parsley, tarragon or dill
- 175 g/6 oz small mushrooms, sliced
- 70 g/2½ oz butter, plus extra for greasing
- 175 g/6 oz cooked peeled prawns
- 40 g/1½ oz plain flour
- 125 ml/4 fl oz double cream
- 1 quantity Perfect Mash (see page 118)
- salt and pepper

1 Preheat the oven to 180°C/350°F/Gas Mark 4. Grease a 1.7-litre/3-pint baking dish with butter.

2 Fold the fish fillets in half and place in the dish. Season well with salt and pepper, pour over the wine and scatter over the herbs.

3 Cover with foil and bake for 15 minutes until the fish starts to flake. Strain off the liquid and reserve for the sauce. Increase the oven temperature to 220°C/425°F/Gas Mark 7.

4 Sauté the mushrooms in a frying pan with 15 g/½ oz of the butter and spoon over the fish. Scatter over the prawns.

5 Heat the remaining butter in a saucepan and stir in the flour. Cook for a few minutes without browning, remove from the heat, then add the reserved cooking liquid gradually, stirring well between each addition.

6 Return to the heat and gently bring to the boil, still stirring to ensure a smooth sauce. Add the cream and season to taste with salt and pepper. Pour over the fish in the dish and smooth over the surface.

7 Pile or pipe the mash onto the fish and sauce and bake for 10–15 minutes until golden brown.

GRANDMA'S TIP
Grate dried-up hard and semi-hard cheeses no longer fit for the table and freeze to use later in sauces or as a topping.

Vegetable Cobbler

SERVES 4

INGREDIENTS

- 1 tbsp olive oil
- 1 garlic clove, crushed
- 8 small onions, halved
- 2 celery sticks, sliced
- 225 g/8 oz swede, chopped
- 2 carrots, sliced
- ½ small head of cauliflower, broken into florets
- 225 g/8 oz button mushrooms, sliced
- 400 g/14 oz canned chopped tomatoes
- 55 g/2 oz red lentils, rinsed
- 2 tbsp cornflour
- 3–4 tbsp water
- 300 ml/10 fl oz vegetable stock
- 2 tsp Tabasco sauce
- 2 tsp chopped fresh oregano
- fresh oregano sprigs, to garnish

TOPPING

- 225 g/8 oz self-raising flour, plus extra for dusting
- pinch of salt
- 4 tbsp butter
- 115 g/4 oz grated mature Cheddar cheese
- 2 tsp chopped fresh oregano
- 1 egg, lightly beaten
- 150 ml/5 fl oz milk

1 Preheat the oven to 180°C/350°F/Gas Mark 4. Heat the oil in a large frying pan, add the garlic and onions and cook over a low heat for 5 minutes. Add the celery, swede, carrots and cauliflower and cook for 2–3 minutes.

2 Add the mushrooms, tomatoes and lentils. Place the cornflour and water in a bowl and mix to make a smooth paste. Stir into the frying pan with the stock, Tabasco sauce and oregano. Transfer to an ovenproof dish, cover and bake in the preheated oven for 20 minutes.

3 To make the topping, sift the flour and salt together into a bowl. Add the butter and rub it in, then stir in most of the cheese, reserving some for the topping, and oregano. Beat the egg with the milk in a small bowl and add enough to the dry ingredients to make a soft dough, reserving some for the topping. Knead, then roll out on a lightly floured work surface to 1 cm/½ inch thick. Cut into 5-cm/2-inch rounds.

4 Remove the dish from the oven and increase the temperature to 200°C/400°F/Gas Mark 6. Arrange the dough rounds around the edge of the dish, brush with the remaining egg and milk mixture and sprinkle with the reserved cheese. Return to the oven and cook for a further 10–12 minutes. Garnish with oregano sprigs and serve.

IDEAL WINTER WARMER

Jam Roly-poly

SERVES 6

INGREDIENTS

- 225 g/8 oz self-raising flour
- pinch of salt
- 115 g/4 oz suet
- grated rind of 1 lemon
- 1 tbsp sugar
- 125 ml/4 fl oz mixed
  milk and water
- 4–6 tbsp Classic Strawberry
  Jam (see page 38)
- 2 tbsp milk
- Home-made Vanilla Custard
  (see page 144), to serve

1 Sift the flour into a mixing bowl and add the salt and suet. Mix together well. Stir in the lemon rind and the sugar.

2 Make a well in the centre and add the milk and water mixture to give a light, elastic dough. Knead lightly until smooth. Wrap the dough in clingfilm and leave to rest for 30 minutes.

3 Roll the dough into a rectangle measuring 20 x 25-cm/8 x 10-inches.

4 Spread the Jam over the dough, leaving a 1-cm/½-inch border. Brush the border with the milk and roll up the dough carefully, like a Swiss roll, from one short end. Seal the ends.

5 Wrap the roly-poly loosely in greaseproof paper and then overwrap with foil, sealing the ends well.

6 Place the roly-poly in a steamer over a saucepan of rapidly boiling water and steam for 1½–2 hours, making sure you top up the water from time to time.

7 When cooked, remove from the steamer, unwrap, cut into slices and serve on warmed plates with Custard.

Spotted Dick

SERVES 6

INGREDIENTS

- 225 g/8 oz self-raising flour, plus extra for dusting
- 115 g/4 oz suet
- 55 g/2 oz caster sugar
- 140 g/5 oz currants or raisins
- grated rind of 1 lemon
- 150–175 ml/5–6 fl oz milk
- 2 tsp melted butter, for greasing
- Home-made Vanilla Custard (see page 144), to serve

1 Mix together the flour, suet, sugar, currants and lemon rind in a mixing bowl.

2 Pour in the milk and stir together to give a fairly soft dough.

3 Turn out onto a floured surface and roll into a cylinder. Wrap in greaseproof paper that has been well-greased with the melted butter and seal the ends, allowing room for the pudding to rise. Overwrap with foil and place in a steamer over a saucepan of boiling water.

4 Steam for about 1–1½ hours, checking the water level in the saucepan from time to time.

5 Remove the pudding from the steamer and unwrap. Place on a warmed plate and cut into thick slices. Serve with lots of custard.

GRANDMA'S TIP
Don't go to the supermarket with an empty stomach as you will be more likely to make impulse buys that eat into the family budget.

Sherry Trifle

SERVES 8

INGREDIENTS

FRUIT LAYER
- 100 g/3½ oz trifle sponges
- 150 g/5½ oz Classic
  Strawberry Jam
  (see page 38)
- 250 ml/9 fl oz sherry
- 150 g/5½ oz fresh
  strawberries, hulled
  and sliced
- 400 g/14 oz canned mixed
  fruit, drained
- 1 large banana, sliced

CUSTARD LAYER
- 6 egg yolks
- 50 g/1¾ oz caster sugar
- 500 ml/18 fl oz milk
- 1 tsp vanilla extract

TOPPING
- 300 ml/10 fl oz
  double cream
- 1–2 tbsp caster sugar
- chocolate flakes or curls,
  to decorate

1 Spread the trifle sponges with jam, cut them into bite-sized cubes and arrange in the bottom of a large glass serving bowl. Pour over the sherry and leave for 30 minutes.

2 Combine the strawberries, canned fruit and banana and arrange over the sponges. Cover with clingfilm and chill in the refrigerator for 30 minutes.

3 To make the custard layer, put the egg yolks and sugar into a bowl and whisk together. Pour the milk into a saucepan and heat gently over a low heat. Remove from the heat and gradually stir into the egg mixture, then return the mixture to the pan and stir constantly over a low heat until thickened. Do not boil.

4 Remove from the heat, pour into a bowl and stir in the vanilla extract. Leave to cool for 1 hour. Spread the custard over the trifle sponge and fruit mixture, cover with clingfilm and chill in the refrigerator for 2 hours.

5 To make the topping, whip the cream in a bowl and stir in sugar to taste. Spread over the trifle, then scatter over the chocolate flakes. Cover with clingfilm and chill in the refrigerator for at least 2 hours before serving.

GRANDMA'S TIP
Instead of trifle sponges, you could use macaroon biscuits, sponge fingers or even sliced Swiss roll.

Apple Pie

SERVES 6

INGREDIENTS

PASTRY

- 350 g/12 oz plain flour
- pinch of salt
- 85 g/3 oz butter or
  margarine, cut into
  small pieces
- 85 g/3 oz lard or white
  vegetable fat, cut into
  small pieces
- about 6 tbsp cold water
- beaten egg or milk,
  for glazing

FILLING

- 750 g–1 kg/1 lb 10 oz–
  2 lb 4 oz cooking apples,
  peeled, cored and sliced
- 125 g/4½ oz soft light
  brown sugar or caster sugar,
  plus extra for sprinkling
- ½–1 tsp ground
  cinnamon, mixed spice
  or ground ginger
- 1–2 tbsp water (optional)

1 To make the pastry, sift the flour and salt into a mixing bowl. Add the butter and lard and rub in with your fingertips until the mixture resembles fine breadcrumbs. Add the water and gather the mixture together into a dough. Wrap the dough and chill in the refrigerator for 30 minutes.

2 Preheat the oven to 220°C/425°F/ Gas Mark 7. Roll out almost two thirds of the pastry thinly and use to line a deep 23-cm/ 9-inch pie plate or pie tin.

3 To make the filling, mix the apples with the sugar and spice and pack into the pastry case. Add the water if needed, particularly if the apples are not very juicy.

4 Roll out the remaining pastry to form a lid. Dampen the edges of the pie rim with water and position the lid, pressing the edges firmly together. Trim and crimp the edges.

5 Using the trimmings, cut out leaves or other shapes to decorate the top of the pie. Dampen and attach. Glaze the top of the pie with the beaten egg and make one or two slits in the top.

6 Place the pie on a baking tray and bake in the preheated oven for 20 minutes, then reduce the oven temperature to 180°C/350°F/Gas Mark 4 and bake for a further 30 minutes, or until the pastry is a light golden brown. Serve hot or cold, sprinkled with sugar.

GRANDMA'S TIP
Prevent apples discoloring
by placing the peeled slices
in a bowl of water with
the juice of 1 lemon added.

Mini Yorkshire Puddings

MAKES 6 PUDDINGS
INGREDIENTS

- 30 g/1 oz beef dripping or 2 tbsp sunflower oil
- 140 g/5 oz plain flour
- ½ tsp salt
- 2 eggs
- 225 ml/8 fl oz milk

1 Grease six metal pudding moulds with the dripping, then divide the remaining dripping between the moulds. Preheat the oven to 220°C/425°F/Gas Mark 7, placing the moulds in the oven so the dripping can melt while the oven heats.

2 Sift the flour and salt together into a large mixing bowl and make a well in the centre. Break the eggs into the well, add the milk and beat, gradually drawing in the flour from the side to make a smooth batter. Remove the moulds from the oven and spoon in the batter until they are about half full.

3 Bake in the preheated oven for 30–35 minutes, without opening the door, until the puddings are well risen, puffed and golden brown. Serve immediately, as they will collapse if left to stand.

GRANDMA'S TIP
Provide each child with a money box to start a savings habit. Let them keep whatever they find on regular coin hunts down the back of the sofa and under furniture.

Traditional Scones

MAKES 10–12 SCONES

INGREDIENTS

- 450 g/1 lb plain flour, plus extra for dusting
- ½ tsp salt
- 2 tsp baking powder
- 55 g/2 oz butter
- 2 tbsp caster sugar
- 250 ml/9 fl oz milk
- 3 tbsp milk, for glazing
- Classic Strawberry Jam (see page 38) and clotted cream, to serve

1 Preheat the oven to 220°C/425°F/Gas Mark 7. Lightly flour a baking tray.

2 Sift the flour, salt and baking powder into a bowl. Rub in the butter until the mixture resembles breadcrumbs. Stir in the sugar.

3 Make a well in the centre and pour in the milk. Stir in using a round-bladed knife and make a soft dough.

4 Turn the mixture onto a floured work surface and lightly flatten the dough until it is an even thickness, about 1 cm/½ inch. Don't be too heavy-handed – scones need a light touch.

5 Use a 6-cm/2½-inch pastry cutter to cut out the scones, then place them on the prepared baking tray.

6 Glaze with a little milk and bake in the preheated oven for 10–12 minutes, until golden and well risen.

7 Leave to cool on a wire rack and serve freshly baked with Strawberry Jam and clotted cream.

GRANDMA'S TIP
To make fruit scones, add 55 g/2 oz mixed fruit with the sugar. To make wholemeal scones, use wholemeal flour and omit the sugar.

Classic Strawberry Jam

**MAKES ABOUT
1.5 KG/ 3 LB 5 OZ**

INGREDIENTS

- 1.5 kg/3 lb 5 oz ripe, unblemished whole strawberries, hulled and rinsed
- 2 freshly squeezed lemons, juice strained
- 1.5 kg/3 lb 5 oz preserving sugar
- 1 tsp butter

1 Place the strawberries in a preserving pan with the lemon juice, then simmer over a gentle heat for 15–20 minutes, stirring occasionally, until the fruit has collapsed and is very soft.

2 Add the sugar and heat, stirring occasionally, until the sugar has completely dissolved. Add the butter, then bring to the boil and boil rapidly for 10–20 minutes, or until the jam has reached its setting point.

3 Leave to cool for 8–10 minutes, then skim and pot into warmed sterilized jars and immediately cover the tops with waxed discs. When completely cold, cover with cellophane or lids, label and store in a cool place.

GRANDMA'S TIP
Other flavours can be added if liked. Add 2 lightly bruised lemongrass stalks and 4 lightly bruised green cardamom pods. Discard the spices before potting.

Orange & Squash Marmalade

**MAKES ABOUT
2.25 KG/5 LB**

INGREDIENTS

- 900 g/2 lb acorn squash or butternut squash (peeled and deseeded weight), cut into small chunks
- 6 blood oranges, scrubbed
- 150 ml/5 fl oz freshly squeezed lemon juice
- small piece fresh ginger, peeled and grated
- 2 serrano chillies, deseeded and finely sliced
- 1.2 litres/2 pints water
- 1.25 kg/2 lb 12 oz preserving sugar

1 Place the squash in a large saucepan with a tight-fitting lid. Thinly slice two of the oranges without peeling, reserving the pips, and add to the saucepan.

2 Peel the remaining oranges, chop the flesh and add to the pan together with the lemon juice, grated ginger and sliced chillies. Tie up the orange pips in a piece of muslin and add to the pan with the water.

3 Bring to the boil, then reduce the heat, cover and simmer gently for 1 hour, or until the squash and oranges are very soft. If preferred, transfer the mixture to a preserving pan.

4 Add the sugar and heat gently, stirring, until the sugar has completely dissolved. Bring to the boil and boil rapidly for 15 minutes, or until the setting point is reached.

5 Skim, if necessary, then leave to cool for 10 minutes. Pot into warmed sterilized jars and immediately cover the tops with waxed discs. When completely cold, cover with cellophane or lids, label and store in a cool place.

GRANDMA'S TIP
This marmalade is ideal for serving with meat and cheese dishes. The marmalade can also be served warm. Heat gently before serving.

Cherry with Brandy Jam

MAKES ABOUT
2.25 KG/5 LB
INGREDIENTS

- 1.8 kg/4 lb dark cherries, such as Morello, rinsed and stoned
- 125 ml/4 fl oz freshly squeezed lemon juice or 1½ tsp citric or tartaric acid
- 150 ml/5 fl oz water (optional)
- 1.25 kg/2 lb 12 oz granulated sugar
- 1 tsp butter
- 4 tbsp brandy
- 225 ml/8 fl oz liquid pectin

1 Roughly chop the cherries and place in a large preserving pan with the lemon juice. If using citric or tartaric acid, add to the pan with the water. Place the pan over a gentle heat, cover and simmer gently for 20 minutes, or until the cherries have collapsed and are very soft.

2 Add the sugar and heat, stirring frequently, until the sugar has completely dissolved. Add the butter and brandy, bring to the boil and boil rapidly for 3 minutes. Remove from the heat and stir in the pectin.

3 Leave to cool for 10 minutes then pot into warmed sterilized jars and cover the tops with waxed discs. When completely cold, cover with cellophane or lids, label and store in a cool place.

GRANDMA'S TIP
Other spirits or liqueurs can be used in place of the brandy. Try Kirsch, Cointreau or a whisky liqueur.

OLD-FASHIONED COMFORT FOOD

Tomato Soup

SERVES 4

INGREDIENTS

- 55 g/2 oz butter
- 1 onion, finely chopped
- 700 g/1 lb 9 oz tomatoes, finely chopped
- 600 ml/1 pint hot chicken stock or vegetable stock
- pinch of sugar
- 2 tbsp shredded fresh basil leaves, plus extra sprig to garnish
- 1 tbsp chopped fresh parsley
- salt and pepper
- chilli oil, for drizzling (optional)

1 Melt half the butter in a large, heavy-based saucepan. Add the onion and cook over a low heat, stirring occasionally, for 5 minutes, or until softened. Add the tomatoes, season to taste with salt and pepper and cook for 5 minutes.

2 Pour in the hot stock, bring back to the boil, then reduce the heat and cook for 10 minutes.

3 Push the soup through a sieve with the back of a wooden spoon to remove the tomato skins and seeds. Return to the saucepan and stir in the sugar, remaining butter, basil and parsley. Heat through briefly, but do not allow to boil.

4 Ladle into warmed soup bowls. Serve immediately, garnished with a sprig of basil and a drizzle of chilli oil, if using.

HEART WARMING FOOD

Split Pea & Ham Soup

SERVES 6–8

INGREDIENTS

- 500 g/1 lb 2 oz split green peas
- 1 tbsp olive oil
- 1 large onion, finely chopped
- 1 large carrot, finely chopped
- 1 celery stick, finely chopped
- 1 litre/1¾ pints chicken stock
  or vegetable stock
- 1 litre/1¾ pints water
- 225 g/8 oz lean smoked ham,
  finely diced
- ¼ tsp dried thyme
- ¼ tsp dried marjoram
- 1 bay leaf
- salt and pepper

1 Rinse the peas under cold running water. Put them in a saucepan and cover generously with water. Bring to the boil and boil for 3 minutes, skimming off the foam from the surface. Drain the peas.

2 Heat the oil in a large saucepan over a medium heat. Add the onion and cook for 3–4 minutes, stirring occasionally, until just softened. Add the carrot and celery and continue cooking for 2 minutes.

3 Add the peas, pour over the stock and water and stir to combine.

4 Bring just to the boil and stir the ham into the soup. Add the thyme, marjoram and bay leaf. Reduce the heat, cover and cook gently for 1–1½ hours, until the ingredients are very soft. Remove the bay leaf.

5 Taste and adjust the seasoning. Ladle into warmed soup bowls and serve.

Hearty Beef Stew

SERVES 4

INGREDIENTS

- 1.3 kg/3 lb boneless braising steak, cut into 5-cm/2-inch pieces
- 2 tbsp vegetable oil
- 2 onions, cut into 2.5-cm/1-inch pieces
- 3 tbsp plain flour
- 3 garlic cloves, finely chopped
- 1 litre/1¾ pints beef stock
- 3 carrots, cut into 2.5-cm/1-inch lengths
- 2 celery sticks, cut into 2.5-cm/1-inch lengths
- 1 tbsp tomato ketchup
- 1 bay leaf
- ¼ tsp dried thyme
- ¼ tsp dried rosemary
- 900 g/2 lb Maris Piper potatoes, cut into large chunks
- salt and pepper

1 Season the steak very generously with salt and pepper. Heat the oil in a large flameproof casserole over a high heat. When the oil begins to smoke slightly, add the steak, in batches, if necessary, and cook, stirring frequently, for 5–8 minutes, until well browned. Using a slotted spoon, transfer to a bowl.

2 Reduce the heat to medium, add the onions to the casserole and cook, stirring occasionally, for 5 minutes, until translucent. Stir in the flour and cook, stirring constantly, for 2 minutes. Add the garlic and cook for 1 minute. Whisk in 225 ml/8 fl oz of the stock and cook, scraping up all the sediment from the base of the casserole, then stir in the remaining stock and add the

carrots, celery, tomato ketchup, bay leaf, thyme, rosemary and 1 teaspoon of salt. Return the steak to the casserole.

3 Bring back to a gentle simmer, cover and cook over a low heat for 1 hour. Add the potatoes, re-cover the casserole and simmer for a further 30 minutes. Remove the lid, increase the heat to medium and cook, stirring occasionally, for a further 30 minutes, or until the meat and vegetables are tender.

4 If the stew becomes too thick, add a little more stock or water and adjust the seasoning, if necessary. Leave to stand for 15 minutes before serving.

GRANDMA'S TIP
Braising steak is a term used for several cuts of beef that are suited to long, slow cooking. Look for a marbling of fat through the meat, which will break down during cooking and add flavour.

Bangers & Mash with Onion Gravy

SERVES 4

INGREDIENTS

- 1 tbsp olive oil
- 8 good-quality sausages

ONION GRAVY
- 3 onions, halved and thinly sliced
- 70 g/2½ oz butter
- 125 ml/4 fl oz Marsala or port
- 125 ml/4 fl oz vegetable stock
- salt and pepper

MASH
- 900 g/2 lb floury potatoes, such as King Edward, Maris Piper or Desirée, peeled and cut into chunks
- 55 g/2 oz butter
- 3 tbsp hot milk
- 2 tbsp chopped fresh parsley
- salt and pepper

1 Place a frying pan over a low heat with the oil and add the sausages. (Alternatively, you may wish to grill the sausages.) Cover the pan and cook for 25–30 minutes, turning the sausages from time to time, until browned all over.

2 Meanwhile, prepare the onion gravy by placing the onions in a frying pan with the butter and frying over a low heat until soft, stirring constantly. Continue to cook for around 30 minutes, or until the onions are brown and have started to caramelize.

3 Pour in the Marsala and stock and continue to bubble away until the onion gravy is really thick. Season to taste with salt and pepper.

4 To make the mash, bring a large saucepan of lightly salted water to the boil, add the potatoes, bring back to the boil and cook for 15–20 minutes. Drain well and mash with a potato masher until smooth. Season to taste with salt and pepper, add the butter, milk and parsley and stir well.

5 Serve the sausages immediately with the mash, and the onion gravy spooned over the top.

GRANDMA'S TIP
When cooking lots of sausages, thread them on to skewers before putting them under the grill or on the barbecue to make them easy to turn.

Steak Sandwiches

MAKES 4 SANDWICHES

INGREDIENTS

- 8 slices thick white or brown bread
- butter, for spreading
- 2 handfuls mixed salad leaves
- 3 tbsp olive oil
- 2 onions, thinly sliced
- 675 g/1 lb 8 oz rump or sirloin steak, about 2.5 cm/1 inch thick
- 1 tbsp Worcestershire sauce
- 2 tbsp wholegrain mustard
- 2 tbsp water
- salt and pepper

1 Spread each slice of bread with some butter and add a few salad leaves to the bottom slices.

2 Heat 2 tablespoons of the oil in a large, heavy-based frying pan over a medium heat. Add the onions and cook, stirring occasionally, for 10–15 minutes until softened and golden brown. Using a slotted spoon, transfer to a plate and set aside.

3 Increase the heat to high and add the remaining oil to the pan. Add the steak, season to taste with pepper and cook quickly on both sides to seal. Reduce the heat to medium and cook, turning once, for 2½–3 minutes each side for rare or 3½–5 minutes each side for medium. Transfer the steak to a plate.

4 Add the Worcestershire sauce, mustard and water to the pan and stir to deglaze by scraping any sediment from the base of the pan. Return the onions to the pan, season to taste with salt and pepper and mix well.

5 Thinly slice the steak across the grain, divide between the four bottom slices of bread and cover with the onions. Cover with the top slices of bread and press down gently. Serve immediately.

FEEL-BETTER FOOD

Ham & Cheese Sandwich

MAKES 1 SANDWICH

INGREDIENTS

- 2 slices country-style bread, such as white Italian bread, thinly sliced
- 20 g/¾ oz butter, at room temperature
- 55 g/2 oz Gruyère cheese, grated
- 1 slice cooked ham, trimmed to fit the bread, if necessary

1 Thinly spread each slice of bread on one side with butter, then put one slice on the work surface, buttered side down. Sprinkle half the cheese over, taking it to the edge of the bread, then add the ham and top with the remaining cheese. Add the other slice of bread, buttered side up, and press down.

2 Heat a heavy-based frying pan, ideally non-stick, over a medium–high heat until hot. Reduce the heat to medium, add the sandwich and fry on one side for 2–3 minutes, until golden brown.

3 Flip the sandwich over and fry on the other side for 2–3 minutes, until all the cheese is melted and the bread is golden brown. Cut the sandwich in half diagonally and serve immediately.

QUICK & SIMPLE FIX

Tuna Melts

INGREDIENTS

- 4 slices sourdough bread
- 400 g/14 oz canned tuna, drained and flaked
- 4 tbsp mayonnaise, or to taste
- 1 tbsp Dijon mustard or wholegrain mustard, plus extra, to taste
- 4 spring onions, trimmed and chopped
- 2 tbsp dill pickle or sweet pickle, to taste
- 1 hard-boiled egg, shelled and finely chopped
- 1 small carrot, peeled and grated
- 1 tbsp capers in brine, rinsed and coarsely chopped
- 2 tbsp chopped parsley or chives
- handful of lettuce leaves
- 8 thin slices red Cheddar cheese
- salt and pepper

1 Preheat the grill to high and position the grill rack about 10 cm/4 inches from the heat source. Line a baking sheet with foil and set aside. Place the bread on the grill rack and toast for 2 minutes on each side, or until crisp and lightly browned.

2 Meanwhile, put the tuna in a bowl with the mayonnaise and mustard and beat together to break up the tuna. Add the spring onions, pickle, egg, carrot, capers, and salt and pepper to taste and beat together, adding extra mayonnaise or mustard to taste. Stir in the parsley.

3 Put the toast on the foil-lined baking sheet and top each slice with a lettuce leaf. Divide the tuna salad between the slices of toast and spread out. Top each sandwich with cheese slices, cut to fit.

4 Place under the grill and grill for 2 minutes, or until the cheese is melted and very lightly browned. Cut each tuna melt into four slices, transfer to a plate and serve immediately.

Pasta with Pesto

INGREDIENTS

• 450 g/1 lb dried tagliatelle
• fresh basil leaves, to garnish
• salt

PESTO
• 2 garlic cloves
• 25 g/1 oz pine kernels
• 115 g/4 oz fresh basil leaves
• 55 g/2 oz freshly grated
  Parmesan cheese
• 125 ml/4 fl oz olive oil
• salt

1 To make the pesto, put the garlic, pine kernels, a large pinch of salt and the basil into a mortar and pound to a paste with a pestle. Transfer to a bowl and gradually work in the cheese with a wooden spoon, then add the olive oil to make a thick, creamy sauce. Taste and adjust the seasoning, if necessary.

2 Alternatively, put the garlic, pine kernels and a large pinch of salt into a blender or food processor and process briefly. Add the basil and process to a paste. With the motor still running, gradually add the olive oil. Scrape into a bowl and beat in the cheese. Season to taste with salt.

3 Bring a large saucepan of lightly salted water to the boil. Add the pasta, bring back to the boil and cook for 8–10 minutes, or until tender but still firm to the bite.

4 Drain well, return to the saucepan and toss with half the pesto, then divide between warmed serving plates and top with the remaining pesto. Garnish with the basil leaves and serve.

GRANDMA'S TIP
Try replacing the traditional tomato sauce on your home-made pizza with pesto, top with mozzarella and bake.

Macaroni Cheese

SERVES 4

INGREDIENTS

- 250 g/9 oz dried macaroni pasta
- 55 g/2 oz butter, plus extra for cooking the pasta
- 600 ml/1 pint milk
- ½ tsp grated nutmeg
- 55 g/2 oz plain flour
- 200 g/7 oz mature Cheddar cheese, grated
- 55 g/2 oz Parmesan cheese, grated
- 200 g/7 oz baby spinach
- salt and pepper

1 Cook the macaroni according to the instructions on the packet. Remove from the heat, drain, add a small knob of butter to keep it soft, return to the saucepan and cover to keep warm.

2 Put the milk and nutmeg into a saucepan over a low heat and heat until warm, but don't boil. Put the butter into a heavy-based saucepan over a low heat, melt the butter, add the flour and stir to make a roux. Cook gently for 2 minutes. Add the milk a little at a time, whisking it into the roux, then cook for about 10–15 minutes to make a loose, custard-style sauce.

3 Add three quarters of the Cheddar cheese and Parmesan cheese and stir through until they have melted in, then add the spinach, season with salt and pepper and remove from the heat.

4 Preheat the grill to high. Put the macaroni into a shallow heatproof dish, then pour the sauce over. Scatter the remaining cheese over the top and place the dish under the preheated grill. Grill until the cheese begins to brown, then serve.

GRANDMA'S TIP
You can add texture to this by sprinkling some wholemeal breadcrumbs over the cheese before placing under the grill.

Tuna & Pasta Casserole

SERVES 4–6

INGREDIENTS

- 200 g/7 oz dried ribbon egg pasta, such as tagliatelle
- 25 g/1 oz butter
- 55 g/2 oz fine fresh breadcrumbs
- 400 ml/14 fl oz canned condensed cream of mushroom soup
- 125 ml/4 fl oz milk
- 2 celery sticks, chopped
- 1 red pepper, deseeded and chopped
- 1 green pepper, deseeded and chopped
- 140 g/5 oz mature Cheddar cheese, coarsely grated
- 2 tbsp chopped fresh parsley
- 200 g/7 oz canned tuna in oil, drained and flaked
- salt and pepper

1 Preheat the oven to 200°C/400°F/Gas Mark 6. Bring a large saucepan of lightly salted water to the boil. Add the pasta, bring back to the boil and cook for 2 minutes less than specified on the packet instructions.

2 Meanwhile, melt the butter in a separate small saucepan. Stir in the breadcrumbs, then remove from the heat and set aside.

3 Drain the pasta well and set aside. Pour the soup into the pasta pan, set over a medium heat, then stir in the milk, celery, red pepper, green pepper, half the cheese and all the parsley.

4 Add the tuna and gently stir in so that the flakes don't break up. Season to taste with salt and pepper. Heat just until small bubbles appear around the edge of the mixture – do not boil.

5 Stir the pasta into the pan and use two forks to mix all the ingredients together. Spoon the mixture into an ovenproof dish that is also suitable for serving and spread it out.

6 Stir the remaining cheese into the buttered breadcrumbs, then sprinkle over the top of the pasta mixture. Bake in the preheated oven for 20–25 minutes, until the topping is golden. Remove from the oven, then leave to stand for 5 minutes before serving straight from the dish.

DELICIOUS & ECONOMICAL

Cauliflower Cheese

SERVES 4

INGREDIENTS

- 1 cauliflower, trimmed and cut into florets (675 g/ 1 lb 8 oz prepared weight)
- 40 g/1½ oz butter
- 40 g/1½ oz plain flour
- 450 ml/16 fl oz milk
- 115 g/4 oz Cheddar cheese, finely grated
- whole nutmeg, for grating
- 1 tbsp grated Parmesan cheese
- salt and pepper

1 Bring a saucepan of lightly salted water to the boil, add the cauliflower, bring back to the boil and cook for 4–5 minutes. It should still be firm. Drain, place in a warmed 1.4-litre/2½-pint gratin dish and keep warm.

2 Melt the butter in the rinsed-out pan over a medium heat and stir in the flour. Cook for 1 minute, stirring constantly.

3 Remove the pan from the heat and gradually stir in the milk until you have a smooth consistency.

4 Return the pan to a low heat and continue to stir while the sauce comes to the boil and thickens. Reduce the heat and simmer gently, stirring constantly, for about 3 minutes, until the sauce is creamy and smooth.

5 Remove from the heat and stir in the Cheddar cheese and a good grating of the nutmeg. Taste and season well with salt and pepper. Meanwhile, preheat the grill to high.

6 Pour the hot sauce over the cauliflower, top with the Parmesan cheese and place under the preheated grill to brown. Serve immediately.

GRANDMA'S TIP
Using a mixture of cauliflower and broccoli will give a more colourful dish. You can make it even more substantial by adding some fried sliced onions and fried bacon pieces before pouring over the sauce.

Chicken & Broccoli Casserole

SERVES 4

INGREDIENTS

- 400 g/14 oz broccoli florets
- 40 g/1½ oz butter
- 1 onion, thinly sliced
- 350 g/12 oz cooked chicken, cut into bite-sized chunks
- 100 g/3½ oz crème fraîche
- 200 ml/7 fl oz chicken stock
- 25 g/1 oz fresh white breadcrumbs
- 55 g/2 oz Gruyère or Emmenthal cheese, grated
- salt and pepper

1 Preheat the oven to 200°C/400°F/Gas Mark 6. Bring a saucepan of lightly salted water to the boil, add the broccoli and cook for 5 minutes until tender. Drain well.

2 Meanwhile, melt 25g/1 oz of the butter in a frying pan, add the onion and stir-fry over a medium heat for 3–4 minutes until soft.

3 Layer the broccoli, onion and chicken in a 1.5-litre/2¾-pint ovenproof dish and season well with salt and pepper. Pour over the crème fraîche and stock.

4 Melt the remaining butter in a small saucepan and stir in the breadcrumbs. Mix with the cheese and sprinkle over the dish.

5 Place the dish on a baking sheet in the preheated oven and bake for 20–25 minutes until golden brown and bubbling. Serve hot.

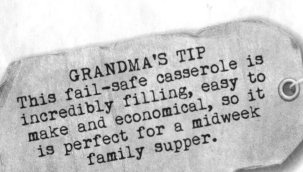

GRANDMA'S TIP
This fail-safe casserole is incredibly filling, easy to make and economical, so it is perfect for a midweek family supper.

Chicken Pot Pie

SERVES 6

INGREDIENTS

- 1 tbsp olive oil
- 225 g/8 oz button mushrooms, sliced
- 1 onion, finely chopped
- 350 g/12 oz carrots, sliced
- 115 g/4 oz celery, sliced
- 1 litre/1¾ pints chicken stock
- 85 g/3 oz butter
- 55 g/2 oz plain flour, plus extra for dusting
- 900 g/2 lb skinless, boneless chicken breasts, cut into 2.5-cm/1-inch cubes
- 115 g/4 oz frozen peas
- 1 tsp chopped fresh thyme or a pinch of dried thyme
- 675 g/1 lb 8 oz shortcrust pastry, thawed, if frozen
- 1 egg, lightly beaten
- salt and pepper

1 Heat the olive oil in a large saucepan over a medium heat. Add the mushrooms and onion and cook, stirring frequently, for about 8 minutes, until golden. Add the carrots, celery and half the stock and bring to the boil. Reduce the heat to low and simmer for 12–15 minutes, until the vegetables are almost tender.

2 Melt the butter in another large saucepan over a medium heat. Whisk in the flour and cook, stirring constantly, for 4 minutes, until the flour is light tan in colour. Gradually whisk in the remaining chicken stock. Reduce the heat to medium–low and simmer, stirring, until thickened.

3 Stir in the vegetable mixture, add the chicken, peas and thyme and season with salt and pepper. Bring back to a simmer and cook, stirring constantly, for 5 minutes. Taste and adjust the seasoning, if necessary, and remove from the heat.

4 Preheat the oven to 200°C/400°F/Gas Mark 6.

5 Divide the filling between six large ramekins, filling them to within 1 cm/½ inch of the top. Roll out the pastry on a lightly floured work surface and cut out six rounds 2.5 cm/1 inch larger than the diameter of the ramekins.

6 Put the rounds on top of the filling, then fold over 1 cm/½ inch all the way around to make a rim. If you like, pinch with your fingertips to form a crimped edge. Cut a small cross in the centre of each crust.

7 Put the ramekins on a baking sheet and brush the tops with the beaten egg. Bake in the preheated oven for 35–40 minutes, until the pies are golden brown and bubbling. Remove from the oven and leave to cool for 15 minutes before serving.

GRANDMA'S TIP
To quickly thaw filo pastry, separate the sheets and cover each one in clingfilm — leave the sheets to thaw at room temperature for 30 minutes.

Home-made Burgers

MAKES 6 BURGERS
INGREDIENTS

- 1 kg/2 lb 4 oz fresh
  beef mince
- 1 small onion, grated
- 1 tbsp chopped
  fresh parsley
- 2 tsp Worcestershire sauce
- 2 tbsp sunflower oil
- salt and pepper

TO SERVE
- 6 burger buns,
  split and toasted
- lettuce leaves
- tomato slices
- gherkins, sliced
- tomato ketchup

1 Put the beef, onion and parsley into a bowl, add the Worcestershire sauce, season to taste with salt and pepper and mix well with your hands until thoroughly combined.

2 Divide the mixture into six equal portions and shape into balls, then gently flatten into patties. If you have time, chill in the refrigerator for 30 minutes to firm up.

3 Heat the oil in a large frying pan. Add the burgers, in batches, and cook over a medium heat for 5–8 minutes on each side, turning them carefully with a fish slice. Remove from the pan and keep warm while you cook the remaining burgers.

4 Serve in toasted buns with lettuce leaves, tomato slices, gherkins and tomato ketchup.

GRANDMA'S
GUILTY
PLEASURE

GRANDMA'S TIP
Make a large batch and freeze, individually wrapped or stored in a plastic container with baking paper between the burgers to keep them separate.

Pizza Margherita

SERVES 6

INGREDIENTS

PIZZA DOUGH

- 15 g/½ oz easy-blend dried yeast
- 1 tsp sugar
- 250 ml/9 fl oz lukewarm water
- 350 g/12 oz strong white flour, plus extra for dusting
- 1 tsp salt
- 1 tbsp olive oil, plus extra for oiling

TOPPING

- 400 g/14 oz canned chopped tomatoes
- 2 garlic cloves, crushed
- 2 tsp dried basil
- 1 tbsp olive oil
- 2 tbsp tomato purée
- 100 g/3½ oz mozzarella cheese, chopped
- 2 tbsp freshly grated Parmesan cheese
- salt and pepper
- fresh basil leaves, to garnish

1 Place the yeast and sugar in a measuring jug and mix with 50 ml/2 fl oz of the water. Leave the yeast mixture in a warm place for 15 minutes or until frothy.

2 Mix the flour with the salt and make a well in the centre. Add the oil, the yeast mixture and the remaining water. Using a wooden spoon, mix to form a smooth dough.

3 Turn out the dough onto a floured work surface and knead for 4–5 minutes or until smooth.

4 Return the dough to the bowl, cover with a sheet of oiled clingfilm and leave to rise for 30 minutes, or until doubled in size.

5 Knead the dough for 2 minutes. Stretch the dough with your hands or roll out on a floured surface with a rolling pin, then place it on an oiled baking tray or pizza stone, pushing out the edges until even. The dough should be no more than 5 mm/¼ inch thick because it will rise during cooking.

6 Preheat the oven to 200°C/400°F/Gas Mark 6. To make the topping, place the tomatoes, garlic, basil, oil, and salt and pepper to taste in a large frying pan over a medium heat and leave to simmer for 20 minutes or until the sauce has thickened. Stir in the tomato purée and leave to cool slightly.

7 Spread the topping evenly over the pizza base. Top with the mozzarella cheese and Parmesan cheese and bake in the preheated oven for 20–25 minutes. Serve hot, garnished with basil leaves.

PRACTICE MAKES PERFECT

Crab Cakes with Tartare Sauce

MAKES 6 CAKES

INGREDIENTS

- 1 large egg, beaten
- 2 tbsp mayonnaise
- ½ tsp Dijon mustard
- ¼ tsp Worcestershire sauce
- ½ tsp celery salt
- ¼ tsp salt
- pinch of cayenne pepper (optional)
- 40 g/1½ oz cream crackers, finely crushed
- 450 g/1 lb fresh crabmeat
- 85–140 g/3–5 oz fresh breadcrumbs
- 25 g/1 oz unsalted butter
- 1 tbsp vegetable oil
- salad leaves and lemon wedges, to serve

TARTARE SAUCE

- 225 ml/8 fl oz mayonnaise
- 4 tbsp sweet pickle relish
- 1 tbsp very finely chopped onion
- 1 tbsp chopped capers
- 1 tbsp chopped parsley
- 1½ tbsp freshly squeezed lemon juice
- dash of Worcestershire sauce
- few drops of Tabasco sauce (optional)
- salt and pepper

1 To make the crab cakes, whisk together the egg, mayonnaise, mustard, Worcestershire sauce, celery salt, salt and cayenne pepper, if using, in a large bowl until combined. Stir in the cracker crumbs with a spatula, then leave to stand for 5 minutes.

2 Pick over the crabmeat to remove any pieces of shell or cartilage, then gently fold into the mixture, trying to avoid breaking it up too much. Cover the bowl with clingfilm and chill in the refrigerator for at least 1 hour.

3 Meanwhile, make the tartare sauce. Mix together all the ingredients in a bowl and season to taste with salt and pepper. Cover and chill in the refrigerator for at least 1 hour before serving.

4 Sprinkle the breadcrumbs over a large plate until lightly covered. Shape the crab mixture into six even-sized cakes, about 2.5 cm/1 inch thick, placing them on the plate as they are formed. Dust the tops of each crab cake lightly with more breadcrumbs.

5 Melt the butter with the oil in a large frying pan over a medium–high heat. Carefully transfer each crab cake from the plate to the pan using a metal spatula.

6 Cook the crab cakes for 4 minutes on each side, until golden brown. Remove from the pan and drain on kitchen paper. Serve immediately with the tartare sauce, salad leaves and lemon wedges.

Spaghetti alla Carbonara

SERVES 4

INGREDIENTS

- 450 g/ I lb dried spaghetti
- I tbsp olive oil
- 225 g/8 oz rindless pancetta or streaky bacon, chopped
- 4 eggs
- 5 tbsp single cream
- 2 tbsp freshly grated Parmesan cheese
- salt and pepper

1 Bring a large, heavy-based saucepan of lightly salted water to the boil, add the pasta, bring back to the boil and cook for 8–10 minutes, or until tender but still firm to the bite.

2 Meanwhile, heat the oil in a heavy-based frying pan. Add the pancetta and cook over a medium heat, stirring frequently, for 8–10 minutes.

3 Beat the eggs with the cream in a small bowl and season to taste with salt and pepper. Drain the pasta and return it to the saucepan. Tip in the contents of the frying pan, then add the egg mixture and half the cheese. Stir well, then transfer the spaghetti to a warmed serving dish. Serve immediately, sprinkled with the remaining cheese.

GRANDMA'S TIP
Sprinkling salt over spilt red wine prevents the stain spreading, but do not do this on a carpet as you'll never remove the residue. Blot with kitchen paper instead.

FAMOUS FAMILY
DINNERS

Whole Roast Rib of Beef

SERVES 8
INGREDIENTS

- olive oil, for rubbing
- 3-kg/6 lb 8-oz joint of
  well-hung rib of beef
  on the bone
- ½ tbsp plain flour
- 200 ml/7 fl oz strong
  beef stock
- 200 ml/7 fl oz red wine
- salt and pepper

YORKSHIRE PUDDINGS
- 250 g/9 oz plain flour, sifted
- 6 eggs
- ½ tsp salt
- 600 ml/1 pint milk
- 2 tbsp vegetable oil or lard

ROAST POTATOES
- 2 kg/4 lb 8 oz roasting
  potatoes, peeled
- 6 tbsp sunflower oil, goose
  fat or duck fat
- salt and pepper

TO SERVE
- glazed carrots
- steamed broccoli
- horseradish sauce (optional)
- mustard (optional)

1 For the Yorkshire pudding, mix the flour, eggs and salt together in a bowl, then gradually add the milk as you stir with a whisk. When smooth set aside but don't chill.

2 For the roast potatoes, bring a large saucepan of lightly salted water to the boil, add the potatoes, bring back to the boil and cook for 10 minutes. Drain the potatoes and toss them in oil and salt and pepper. Put them in a roasting tin in a single layer.

3 Preheat the oven to 220°C/425°F/Gas Mark 7. Put a 40 x 25-cm/16 x 10-inch roasting tin in the bottom of the oven to warm for the Yorkshire pudding mixture.

4 Rub a generous amount of olive oil and salt and pepper into the beef, then place in a roasting tin. Transfer to the preheated oven and roast for 30 minutes.

5 Reduce the temperature to 160°C/325°F/Gas Mark 3. Transfer the potatoes to the oven and roast with the beef for 60 minutes. Remove the beef from the oven and increase the oven temperature to 220°C/425°F/Gas Mark 7. Cover the beef with foil and leave to rest for at least 30 minutes.

6 To make the Yorkshire pudding, remove the roasting tin from the bottom of the oven and add the vegetable oil. Put it back in the oven for 5 minutes, then remove it and add the Yorkshire pudding batter. Put it back in the hot oven for about 20 minutes.

7 Meanwhile, make the gravy. Remove the beef from the tin and stir the flour into the leftover juices, add the stock and wine, then simmer over a medium heat until reduced by about half.

8 Remove the Yorkshire pudding and divide into eight. Then remove the potatoes from the oven. Cut the rib bones off the meat and carve the beef. Serve with the potatoes, Yorkshire puddings, carrots, broccoli, horseradish sauce and mustard, if liked.

HEART WARMING FOOD

Roast Chicken

SERVES 6

INGREDIENTS

- 2.25 kg/5 lb
  free-range chicken
- 55 g/2 oz butter
- 2 tbsp chopped fresh
  lemon thyme
- 1 lemon, quartered
- 125 ml/4 fl oz white wine
- roasted vegetables, to serve
- salt and pepper

1 Preheat the oven to 220°C/425°F/Gas Mark 7.

2 Make sure the chicken is clean, wiping it inside and out with kitchen paper, then place in a roasting tin.

3 In a bowl, soften the butter with a fork, mix in the thyme and season well with salt and pepper.

4 Butter the chicken all over with the herb butter, inside and out, and place the lemon pieces inside the body cavity. Pour the wine over the chicken.

5 Roast in the centre of the preheated oven for 20 minutes. Reduce the temperature to 190°C/375°F/Gas Mark 5 and continue to roast for a further 1¼ hours, basting frequently. Cover with foil if the skin begins to brown too much. If the liquid in the tin dries out, add a little more wine or water.

6 Test that the chicken is cooked by piercing the thickest part of the leg with a sharp knife or skewer and making sure the juices run clear. Remove from the oven.

7 Place the chicken on a warmed serving plate, cover with foil and leave to rest for 10 minutes before carving.

8 Place the roasting tin on the hob and bubble the pan juices gently over a low heat, until they have reduced and are thick and glossy. Season to taste with salt and pepper.

9 Serve the chicken with the pan juices and roasted vegetables.

GRANDMA'S TIP
To give more depth and a touch of sweetness to the finished dish, add a generous splash of Marsala to the pan juices when reducing them.

Leg of Lamb Pot Roast

SERVES 4

INGREDIENTS

- 1 leg of lamb, weighing 1.6 kg/3 lb 8 oz
- 3–4 fresh rosemary sprigs
- 115 g/4 oz streaky bacon rashers
- 4 tbsp olive oil
- 2–3 garlic cloves, crushed
- 2 onions, sliced
- 2 carrots, sliced
- 2 celery sticks, sliced
- 300 ml/10 fl oz dry white wine
- 1 tbsp tomato purée
- 300 ml/10 fl oz lamb stock or chicken stock
- 3 tomatoes, peeled, quartered and deseeded
- 1 tbsp chopped fresh parsley
- 1 tbsp chopped fresh oregano or marjoram
- salt and pepper
- fresh rosemary sprigs, to garnish

1 Wipe the lamb all over with kitchen paper, trim off any excess fat and season to taste with salt and pepper, rubbing in well. Lay the sprigs of rosemary over the lamb, cover evenly with the bacon and tie in place securely with some kitchen string.

2 Heat the oil in a frying pan over a medium heat, add the lamb and fry for 10 minutes, turning several times. Remove from the pan.

3 Preheat the oven to 160°C/325°F/Gas Mark 3. Transfer the oil from the pan to a large, flameproof casserole, add the garlic and onions and cook for 3–4 minutes, until the onions are beginning to soften. Add the carrots and celery and cook for a further few minutes.

4 Lay the lamb on top of the vegetables and press down to partly submerge. Pour the wine over the lamb, add the tomato purée and simmer for 3–4 minutes. Add the stock, tomatoes and herbs and season to taste with salt and pepper. Bring back to the boil and cook for a further 3–4 minutes.

5 Lightly cover the casserole and cook in the preheated oven for 2–2½ hours until very tender.

6 Remove the lamb from the casserole and, if you like, remove the bacon and herbs together with the string. Keep the lamb warm. Strain the juices, skimming off any excess fat, and serve in a jug. The vegetables may be served around the joint or put in a warmed dish. Garnish with sprigs of rosemary.

IDEAL WINTER WARMER

Roast Gammon

SERVES 6
INGREDIENTS

• 1.3 kg/3 lb boneless
  gammon, pre-soaked
  if necessary
• 2 tbsp Dijon mustard
• 85 g/3 oz demerara sugar
• ½ tsp ground cinnamon
• ½ tsp ground ginger
• 18 whole cloves
• ready-made Cumberland
  sauce, to serve

1 Place the gammon in a large saucepan, cover with cold water and slowly bring to the boil over a gentle heat. Cover the pan and simmer very gently for 1 hour.

2 Preheat the oven to 200°C/400°F/Gas Mark 6.

3 Remove the gammon from the pan and drain. Remove the rind from the gammon and discard. Score the fat into a diamond-shaped pattern with a sharp knife.

4 Spread the mustard over the fat. Mix the sugar and the ground spices together on a plate and roll the gammon in the mixture, pressing down well to coat evenly.

5 Stud the diamond shapes with cloves and place the joint in a roasting tin. Roast in the preheated oven for 20 minutes, until the glaze is a rich golden colour.

6 To serve hot, leave to stand for 20 minutes before carving. If the gammon is to be served cold, it can be cooked a day ahead. Serve with Cumberland sauce.

FEEL-BETTER FOOD

GRANDMA'S TIP
Stock an emergency shelf, out of the reach of children, with candles, matches, torches, a first-aid kit and a list of emergency telephone numbers.

Steak & Chips

SERVES 4

INGREDIENTS

- 4 sirloin steaks, about
  225 g/8 oz each
- 4 tsp Tabasco sauce
- salt and pepper

CHIPS
- 450 g/1 lb potatoes, peeled
- 2 tbsp sunflower oil

- WATERCRESS BUTTER
- 1 bunch of watercress
- 85 g/3 oz unsalted
  butter, softened

1 To make the chips, preheat the oven to 200°C/400°F/Gas Mark 6. Cut the potatoes into thick, even-sized chips. Rinse them under cold running water and then dry well on a clean tea towel. Place in a bowl, add the oil and toss together until coated.

2 Spread the chips on a baking sheet and cook in the preheated oven for 40–45 minutes, turning once, until golden.

3 To make the watercress butter, finely chop enough watercress to fill 4 tablespoons. Place the butter in a small bowl and beat in the chopped watercress with a fork until fully incorporated. Cover with clingfilm and leave to chill in the refrigerator until required.

4 Preheat a griddle pan to high. Sprinkle each steak with 1 teaspoon of the Tabasco sauce, rubbing it in well. Season to taste with salt and pepper.

5 Cook the steaks in the preheated pan for 2½ minutes each side for rare, 4 minutes each side for medium and 6 minutes each side for well done. Transfer to serving plates and serve immediately, topped with the watercress butter and accompanied by the chips.

GRANDMA'S TIP
To test for doneness, press the steak gently with the tip of your finger. Rare should be soft and supple, well done firm, and medium in between.

Pork Chops with Apple Sauce

SERVES 4

INGREDIENTS

- 4 pork rib chops on the bone, each about 3 cm/1¼ inches thick, at room temperature
- 1½ tbsp sunflower oil or rapeseed oil
- salt and pepper

APPLE SAUCE

- 450 g/1 lb cooking apples, such as Bramley, peeled, cored and diced
- 4 tbsp caster sugar, plus extra, if needed
- finely grated zest of ½ lemon
- ½ tbsp lemon juice, plus extra, if needed
- 4 tbsp water
- ¼ tsp ground cinnamon
- knob of butter

1 Preheat the oven to 200°C/400°F/Gas Mark 6.

2 To make the apple sauce, put the apples, sugar, lemon zest, lemon juice and water into a heavy-based saucepan over a high heat and bring to the boil, stirring to dissolve the sugar. Reduce the heat to low, cover and simmer for 15–20 minutes, until the apples are tender and fall apart when you mash them against the side of the pan. Stir in the cinnamon and butter and beat the apples until they are as smooth or chunky as you like. Stir in extra sugar or lemon juice, to taste. Remove the pan from the heat, cover and keep the apple sauce warm.

3 Meanwhile, pat the chops dry and season to taste with salt and pepper. Heat the oil in a large ovenproof frying pan over a medium–high heat. Add the chops and fry for 3 minutes on each side to brown.

4 Transfer the pan to the oven and roast the chops for 7–9 minutes until cooked through and the juices run clear when you cut the chops. Remove the pan from the oven, cover with foil and leave to stand for 3 minutes. Gently reheat the apple sauce, if necessary.

5 Transfer the chops to warmed plates and spoon over the pan juices. Serve immediately, accompanied by the apple sauce.

IMPRESS THE FAMILY

Barbecue-glazed Drumsticks

SERVES 6

INGREDIENTS

- 12 chicken drumsticks, about 1.6 kg/3 lb 8 oz
- 225 ml/8 fl oz barbecue sauce
- 1 tbsp soft light brown sugar
- 1 tbsp cider vinegar
- 1 tsp salt
- ½ tsp pepper
- ½ tsp Tabasco sauce
- vegetable oil, for brushing

1 Using a sharp knife, make two slashes, about 2.5 cm/1 inch apart, into the thickest part of the drumsticks, cutting to the bone. Put the drumsticks into a large, sealable polythene freezer bag.

2 Mix together 4 tablespoons of the barbecue sauce, the sugar, vinegar, salt, pepper and Tabasco sauce in a small bowl. Pour the mixture into the bag, press out most of the air and seal tightly. Shake the bag gently to distribute the sauce evenly and leave to marinate in the refrigerator for at least 4 hours.

3 Preheat the oven to 200°C/400°F/Gas Mark 6. Line a baking sheet with foil and brush lightly with oil.

4 Using tongs, transfer the drumsticks to the prepared baking sheet, spacing them evenly apart. Discard the marinade. Brush both sides of the drumsticks with some of the remaining barbecue sauce.

5 Bake for 15 minutes, then remove from the oven and brush generously with more barbecue sauce. Return to the oven and repeat this process three more times for a total cooking time of 1 hour or until the chicken is tender and the juices run clear when a skewer is inserted into the thickest part of the meat. When done, the chicken will be cooked through with a thick, beautiful glaze.

CHILDREN'S FAVOURITE

Fried Chicken Wings

SERVES 4

INGREDIENTS

- 12 chicken wings
- 1 egg
- 60 ml/ 4 tbsp milk
- 4 heaped tbsp plain flour
- 1 tsp paprika
- 225 g/8 oz breadcrumbs
- 55 g/2 oz butter
- salt and pepper

1 Preheat the oven to 220°C/425°F/Gas Mark 7. Separate the chicken wings into three pieces each. Discard the bony tip. Beat the egg with the milk in a shallow dish. Combine the flour, paprika, and salt and pepper to taste in a separate shallow dish. Place the breadcrumbs in another shallow dish.

2 Dip the chicken pieces into the egg to coat well, then drain and roll in the seasoned flour. Remove, shaking off any excess, then roll the chicken in the breadcrumbs, gently pressing them onto the surface and shaking off any excess.

3 Put the butter in a shallow roasting tin large enough to hold all the chicken pieces in a single layer. Place the tin in the preheated oven and melt the butter. Remove from the oven and arrange the chicken, skin-side down, in the tin. Return to the oven and bake for 10 minutes. Turn and bake for a further 10 minutes, or until the chicken is tender and the juices run clear when a skewer is inserted into the thickest part of the meat.

4 Remove the chicken from the tin. Serve hot or at room temperature.

GRANDMA'S TIP
It's a good idea to let coated or breaded chicken rest for about 5 minutes before cooking. This helps set the coating and bind it to the chicken.

Classic Lasagne

SERVES 6
INGREDIENTS

- 2 tbsp olive oil
- 55 g/2 oz pancetta or rindless streaky bacon, chopped
- 1 onion, chopped
- 1 garlic clove, finely chopped
- 225 g/8 oz fresh beef mince
- 2 celery sticks, chopped
- 2 carrots, chopped
- pinch of sugar
- ½ tsp dried oregano
- 400 g/14 oz canned chopped tomatoes
- 225 g/8 oz dried no-precook lasagne sheets
- 115 g/4 oz freshly grated Parmesan cheese, plus extra for sprinkling
- salt and pepper

CHEESE SAUCE

- 300 ml/10 fl oz milk
- 1 bay leaf
- 6 black peppercorns
- slice of onion
- blade of mace
- 2 tbsp butter
- 3 tbsp plain flour
- 2 tsp Dijon mustard
- 70 g/2½ oz Cheddar cheese, grated
- 70 g/2½ oz Gruyère cheese, grated
- salt and pepper

1 Preheat the oven to 190°C/375°F/Gas Mark 5. Heat the oil in a large, heavy-based saucepan. Add the pancetta and cook over a medium heat, stirring occasionally, for 3 minutes, or until the fat begins to run. Add the onion and garlic and cook, stirring occasionally, for 5 minutes, or until softened.

2 Add the beef and cook, breaking it up with a wooden spoon, until browned all over. Stir in the celery and carrots and cook for 5 minutes. Season to taste with salt and pepper. Add the sugar, oregano and tomatoes. Bring to the boil, reduce the heat to low and simmer for 30 minutes.

3 Meanwhile, make the cheese sauce. Pour the milk into a saucepan and add the bay leaf, peppercorns, onion and mace. Heat gently to just below the boiling point, then remove from the heat, cover and leave to infuse for 10 minutes.

4 Strain the milk into a jug. Melt the butter in a clean saucepan. Sprinkle in the flour and cook over a low heat, stirring constantly, for 1 minute. Remove from the heat and gradually stir in the warm milk. Return to the heat and bring to the boil, stirring. Cook, stirring, until thickened and smooth. Stir in the mustard, Cheddar cheese and Gruyère cheese, then season to taste with salt and pepper.

5 In a large, rectangular ovenproof dish, make alternate layers of meat sauce, lasagne sheets and Parmesan cheese. Pour the cheese sauce over the layers, covering them completely, and sprinkle with Parmesan cheese. Bake in the preheated oven for 30 minutes, or until the top is golden brown and bubbling. Serve immediately.

GRANDMA'S TIP
This dish is quite complicated. To cheat a little, you can buy a ready-made cheese sauce to cut down on the preparation time.

Corned Beef Hash

SERVES 6

INGREDIENTS

- 25 g/1 oz butter
- 1 tbsp vegetable oil
- 675 g/1 lb 8 oz corned beef, cut into small cubes
- 1 onion, diced
- 675 g/1 lb 8 oz potatoes, cut into small cubes
- ¼ tsp paprika
- ¼ tsp garlic powder
- 4 tbsp diced green pepper or jalapeño chillies
- 1 tbsp snipped chives, plus extra to garnish
- salt and pepper
- 6 poached eggs, to serve

1 Put the butter, oil, corned beef and onion into a large, cold, non-stick or heavy-based frying pan. Place the pan over a medium–low heat and cook, stirring occasionally, for 10 minutes.

2 Meanwhile, bring a large saucepan of lightly salted water to the boil, add the potatoes, bring back to the boil and cook for 5–7 minutes, until partially cooked but still very firm. Drain well and add to the frying pan, together with the remaining ingredients.

3 Mix together well and press down lightly with a spatula to flatten. Increase the heat to medium. Every 10 minutes, turn the mixture with a spatula to bring the crusty base up to the top. Do this several times until the mixture is well-browned, the potatoes are crisp-edged and the cubes of meat are caramelized.

4 Taste and adjust the seasoning, if necessary. Transfer to warmed plates and top each with a poached egg. Garnish with chives and serve immediately.

DELICIOUS & ECONOMICAL

GRANDMA'S TIP
Quick to make and delicious to eat, this is perfect served with grilled tomatoes, peas or baked beans. If you don't like corned beef, try using leftover cooked turkey or canned tuna.

Meatloaf

SERVES 6–8

INGREDIENTS

- 100 g/3½ oz carrots, diced
- 55 g/2 oz celery, diced
- 1 onion, diced
- 1 red pepper, deseeded and chopped
- 4 large white mushrooms, sliced
- 25 g/1 oz butter
- 1 tbsp olive oil, plus extra for brushing
- 3 garlic cloves, peeled
- 1 tsp dried thyme
- 2 tsp finely chopped rosemary
- 1 tsp Worcestershire sauce
- 4 tbsp tomato ketchup
- ½ tsp cayenne pepper
- 1.1 kg/2 lb 8 oz beef mince, chilled
- 2 tsp salt
- 1 tsp pepper
- 2 eggs, beaten
- 55 g/2 oz fresh breadcrumbs
- garden peas and Perfect Mash (see page 118), to serve

GLAZE

- 2 tbsp brown sugar
- 2 tbsp tomato ketchup
- 1 tbsp Dijon mustard
- salt

1 Put the vegetables into a food processor and pulse until very finely chopped, scraping down the bowl several times with a spatula.

2 Melt the butter with the oil and garlic in a large frying pan. Add the vegetable mixture and cook over a medium heat, stirring frequently, for about 10 minutes, until most of the moisture has evaporated and the mixture is lightly caramelized.

3 Remove the pan from the heat and stir in the thyme, rosemary, Worcestershire sauce, tomato ketchup and cayenne pepper. Leave to cool to room temperature.

4 Preheat the oven to 160°C/325°F/Gas Mark 3. Lightly brush a shallow roasting tin with olive oil.

5 Put the beef into a large bowl and gently break it up with your fingertips. Add the cooled vegetable mixture, salt, pepper and eggs and mix gently with your fingers for just 30 seconds. Add the breadcrumbs and continue to mix until combined. The less you work the meat, the better the texture of the meatloaf.

6 Put the meatloaf mixture in the centre of the prepared roasting tin, dampen your hands with cold water and shape it into a loaf about 15 cm/6 inches wide by 10 cm/4 inches high. Dampen your hands again and smooth the surface. Bake in the centre of the preheated oven for 30 minutes.

7 Meanwhile, make the glaze. Whisk together the brown sugar, ketchup, Dijon mustard and a pinch of salt in a small bowl.

8 Remove the meatloaf from the oven and spread the glaze evenly over the top with a spoon and spread some down the sides as well. Return to the oven and bake for a further 35–45 minutes, or until the internal temperature reaches 70°C/155°F on a meat thermometer. Remove and leave to rest for at least 15 minutes before slicing thickly to serve with peas and mash.

HEART WARMING FOOD

Spaghetti & Meatballs

SERVES 4

INGREDIENTS

- 2 tbsp olive oil, plus extra for brushing
- 1 onion, finely diced
- 4 garlic cloves, finely chopped
- ½ tsp dried Italian herbs
- ½ day-old ciabatta loaf, crusts removed
- 4 tbsp milk
- 900 g/2 lb beef mince, well chilled
- 2 large eggs, lightly beaten
- 5 tbsp chopped fresh flat-leaf parsley
- 55 g/2 oz Parmesan cheese, grated, plus extra to serve
- 1.5 litres/ 2¾ pints marinara or other ready-made pasta sauce
- 225 ml/8 fl oz water
- 450 g/1 lb thick dried spaghetti
- salt and pepper

1 Heat the olive oil in a saucepan. Add the onion, garlic and a pinch of salt, cover and cook over a medium–low heat for 6–7 minutes, until softened and golden. Remove the pan from the heat, stir in the dried herbs and leave to cool to room temperature.

2 Tear the bread into small chunks and put into a food processor, in batches depending on the size of the machine. Pulse to make fine breadcrumbs – you'll need 140 g/5 oz in total. Put the crumbs into a bowl, toss with the milk and leave to soak for 10 minutes.

3 Preheat the oven to 220°C/425°F/Gas Mark 7. Brush a baking sheet with oil.

4 Put the beef, eggs, parsley, cheese, breadcrumbs, cooled onion mixture, 2 teaspoons of salt and 1 teaspoon of pepper into a bowl. Mix well with your hands until thoroughly combined.

5 Dampen your hands and roll pieces of the mixture into balls about the size of a golf ball. Put them on the prepared tray and bake in the preheated oven for 20 minutes. Meanwhile, pour the pasta sauce into a saucepan, stir in the water and bring to a simmering point. When the meatballs are done, transfer them into the hot sauce, reduce the heat to very low, cover and simmer gently for 45 minutes.

6 Bring a large saucepan of lightly salted water to the boil, add the spaghetti, curling it around the pan as it softens. Bring back to the boil and cook for 10–12 minutes, until tender but still firm to the bite.

7 Drain the spaghetti in a colander and tip into a large serving dish. Ladle some of the sauce from the meatballs over it and toss to coat. Top with the meatballs and the remaining sauce, sprinkle with cheese and serve immediately.

GRANDMA'S TIP
For the best flavour, store tomatoes in a basket in a cool place where air can circulate, rather than in the refrigerator.

Fish & Chips with Mushy Peas

SERVES 4

INGREDIENTS

- vegetable oil, for deep-frying
- 6 large floury potatoes, such as King Edward, Maris Piper or Desirée, cut into chips
- 4 thick cod fillets, about 175 g/6 oz each
- flour, for dusting
- salt and pepper

BATTER

- 225 g/8 oz self-raising flour
- ½ tsp salt
- 300 ml/10 fl oz cold lager

MUSHY PEAS

- 350 g/12 oz frozen peas
- 30 g/1 oz butter
- 2 tbsp single cream
- salt and pepper

1 To make the batter, sift the flour into a bowl with the salt and whisk in most of the lager. Check the consistency and add the remaining lager; it should be thick, like double cream. Chill in the refrigerator for half an hour.

2 To make the mushy peas, bring a large saucepan of lightly salted water to the boil, add the peas, bring back to the boil and cook for 3 minutes. Drain and mash to a thick purée, then add the butter and cream and season to taste with salt and pepper. Set aside and keep warm while cooking the fish.

3 Heat the oil to 120°C/250°F in a thermostatically controlled deep fat fryer or in a large saucepan using a thermometer. Preheat the oven to 150°C/300°F/Gas Mark 2.

4 Add the chips to the oil and fry for about 8–10 minutes, until softened but not coloured. Remove from the oil, drain on kitchen paper and place in a dish in the preheated oven. Increase the temperature of the oil to 180°C/350°F.

5 Season the fish to taste with salt and pepper and dust lightly with a little flour. Dip one fillet in the batter and coat thickly.

6 Carefully place the fillet in the hot oil and repeat with the other fillets (you may need to do this in batches). Cook for 8–10 minutes, turning halfway through. Remove the fish from the oil, drain and keep warm.

7 Reheat the oil to 180°C/350°F and recook the chips for a further 2–3 minutes until golden brown. Drain and season to taste with salt and pepper. Serve immediately with the mushy peas.

GRANDMA'S TIP
Avoid overcrowding food in a deep fat fryer or saucepan, as it will make the temperature of the oil drop. This increases the oil absorption, resulting in a soggy batter.

Poached Salmon

SERVES 6

INGREDIENTS

- 1 whole salmon (head on), about 2.7 kg/6 lb to 3.6 kg/ 8 lb prepared weight
- 3 tbsp salt
- 3 bay leaves
- 10 black peppercorns
- 1 onion, peeled and sliced
- 1 lemon, sliced
- lemon wedges, to serve

1 Wipe the salmon thoroughly inside and out with kitchen paper, then use the back of a cook's knife to remove any scales that might still be on the skin. Remove the fins with a pair of scissors and trim the tail. Some people prefer to cut off the head but it is traditionally served with it on.

2 Place the salmon on the two-handled rack that comes with a fish kettle, then place it in the kettle. Fill the kettle with enough cold water to cover the salmon adequately. Sprinkle over the salt, bay leaves and peppercorns and scatter in the onion and lemon slices.

3 Place the kettle over a low heat, over two burners, and bring just to the boil very slowly.

4 Cover and simmer very gently. To serve cold, simmer for 2 minutes only, remove from the heat and leave to cool in the water for about 2 hours with the lid on. To serve hot, simmer for 6–8 minutes and leave to stand in the hot water for 15 minutes before removing. Serve with lemon wedges for squeezing over.

IMPRESS THE FAMILY

Asparagus & Tomato Tart

SERVES 4
INGREDIENTS

- butter, for greasing
- 375 g/13 oz ready-made shortcrust pastry, thawed, if frozen
- 1 bunch thin asparagus spears
- 250 g/9 oz spinach leaves
- 3 large eggs, beaten
- 150 ml/5 fl oz double cream
- 1 garlic clove, crushed
- 10 small cherry tomatoes, halved
- handful fresh basil, chopped
- 25 g/1 oz grated Parmesan cheese
- salt and pepper

1 Preheat the oven to 190°C/375°F/Gas Mark 5. Grease a 25–30-cm/10–12-inch tart tin with butter, then roll out the pastry and use to line the tin.

2 Cut off any excess pastry, prick the base with a fork, cover with a piece of greaseproof paper and fill with baking beans, then blind-bake the base in the preheated oven for 20–30 minutes until lightly browned. Remove from the oven and leave to cool slightly. Reduce the oven temperature to 180°C/350°F/Gas Mark 4.

3 Meanwhile, bend the asparagus spears until they snap, and discard the woody bases. Bring a large saucepan of lightly salted water to the boil, add the asparagus and blanch for 1 minute, then remove and drain. Add the spinach to the boiling water, then remove immediately and drain very well.

4 Mix the eggs, cream and garlic together and season to taste with salt and pepper. Lay the blanched spinach at the bottom of the pastry base, add the asparagus and tomatoes, cut side up, in any arrangement you like, scatter over the basil, then pour the egg mixture on top.

5 Transfer to the oven and bake for about 35 minutes, or until the filling has set nicely. Sprinkle the cheese on top and leave to cool to room temperature before serving.

GRANDMA'S TIP
This is a great dish to make for summer picnics and garden parties. The ingredients are interchangeable with other crisp spring and summer vegetables.

Chilli Bean Stew

SERVES 4–6

INGREDIENTS

- 2 tbsp olive oil
- 1 onion, chopped
- 2–4 garlic cloves, chopped
- 2 fresh red chillies, deseeded and sliced
- 225 g/8 oz canned kidney beans, drained and rinsed
- 225 g/8 oz canned cannellini beans, drained and rinsed
- 225 g/8 oz canned chickpeas, drained and rinsed
- 1 tbsp tomato purée
- 700–850 ml/1¼–1½ pints vegetable stock
- 1 red pepper, deseeded and chopped
- 4 tomatoes, chopped
- 175 g/6 oz shelled fresh broad beans
- 1 tbsp chopped fresh coriander
- paprika, to garnish
- soured cream, to serve

1 Heat the oil in a large, heavy-based saucepan with a tight-fitting lid. Add the onion, garlic and chillies and cook, stirring frequently, for 5 minutes until soft.

2 Add the kidney beans, cannellini beans and chickpeas. Blend the tomato purée with a little of the stock and pour over the bean mixture, then add the remaining stock.

3 Bring to the boil, then reduce the heat and simmer for 10–15 minutes. Add the red pepper, tomatoes and broad beans.

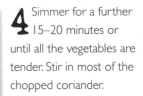

4 Simmer for a further 15–20 minutes or until all the vegetables are tender. Stir in most of the chopped coriander.

5 Serve topped with spoonfuls of soured cream and garnished with chopped coriander and a pinch of paprika.

GRANDMA'S TIP
Look out for canned beans in water, instead of those with added salt and sugar, as they will be healthier for you.

FAIL-SAFE SIDES & SUNDRIES

Roast Potatoes

SERVES 6

INGREDIENTS

- 1.3 kg/3 lb large floury potatoes, such as King Edward, Maris Piper or Desirée, peeled and cut into even-sized chunks
- 3 tbsp dripping, goose fat, duck fat or olive oil
- salt

1 Preheat the oven to 220°C/425°F/Gas Mark 7.

2 Bring a large saucepan of lightly salted water to the boil, add the potatoes, bring back to the boil and cook for 5–7 minutes. The potatoes should still be firm. Remove from the heat.

3 Meanwhile, add the dripping to a roasting tin and place the tin in the preheated oven.

4 Drain the potatoes well and return them to the saucepan. Cover with the lid and firmly shake the pan so that the surface of the potatoes is roughened to help give a much crisper texture.

5 Remove the roasting tin from the oven and carefully tip the potatoes into the hot oil. Baste them to ensure they are all coated with the oil.

6 Roast at the top of the oven for 45–50 minutes until they are browned all over and thoroughly crisp. Turn the potatoes and baste again only once during the process or the crunchy edges will be destroyed.

7 Carefully transfer the potatoes from the roasting tin into a warmed serving dish. Sprinkle with a little salt and serve immediately.

GRANDMA'S GUILTY PLEASURE

Sweet & Sour Red Cabbage

SERVES 6–8

INGREDIENTS

- I red cabbage, about 750 g/1 lb 10 oz
- 2 tbsp olive oil
- 2 onions, finely sliced
- I garlic clove, chopped
- 2 small cooking apples, peeled, cored and sliced
- 2 tbsp muscovado sugar
- ½ tsp ground cinnamon
- I tsp crushed juniper berries
- whole nutmeg, for grating
- 2 tbsp red wine vinegar
- grated rind and juice of I orange
- 2 tbsp redcurrant jelly
- salt and pepper

1 Cut the cabbage into quarters, remove the centre stalk and finely shred the leaves.

2 Heat the oil in a large saucepan over a medium heat and add the cabbage, onions, garlic and apples. Stir in the sugar, cinnamon and juniper berries and grate a quarter of the nutmeg into the pan.

3 Pour over the vinegar and orange juice and add the orange rind.

4 Stir well and season to taste with salt and pepper. The pan will be quite full but the volume of the cabbage will reduce during cooking.

5 Cook over a medium heat, stirring occasionally, until the cabbage is just tender but still has 'bite'. This will take 10–15 minutes, depending on how finely the cabbage is sliced.

6 Stir in the redcurrant jelly, then taste and adjust the seasoning, adding salt and pepper if necessary. Serve immediately.

GRANDMA'S TIP
This is the perfect winter dish and is the classic accompaniment to roast pork. It also goes well with ham at Christmas, or sausages, any day of the week.

Perfect Mash

SERVES 4

INGREDIENTS

- 900 g/2 lb floury potatoes, such as King Edward, Maris Piper or Desirée, peeled and cut into even-sized chunks
- 55 g/2 oz butter
- 3 tbsp hot milk
- salt and pepper

1 Bring a large saucepan of lightly salted water to the boil, add the potatoes, bring back to the boil and cook for 20–25 minutes until they are tender. Test with the point of a knife, but do make sure you test right to the middle to avoid lumps.

2 Remove the pan from the heat and drain the potatoes. Return the potatoes to the hot pan and mash with a potato masher until smooth.

3 Add the butter and continue to mash until it is all mixed in, then add the milk (it is better hot because the potatoes absorb it more quickly to produce a creamier mash).

4 Taste the mash and season with salt and pepper as necessary. Serve immediately.

FEEL-BETTER FOOD

Asparagus with Lemon Butter Sauce

SERVES 4

INGREDIENTS

• 800 g/1 lb 12 oz asparagus
  spears, trimmed
• 1 tbsp olive oil
• salt and pepper

LEMON BUTTER SAUCE

• juice of ½ lemon
• 2 tbsp water
• 100 g/3½ oz butter,
  cut into cubes

1 Preheat the oven to 200°C/400°F/Gas Mark 6.

2 Lay the asparagus spears in a single layer on a large baking sheet. Drizzle over the oil, season to taste with salt and pepper and roast in the preheated oven for 10 minutes, or until just tender.

3 Meanwhile, make the lemon butter sauce. Pour the lemon juice into a saucepan and add the water. Heat for a minute or so, then slowly add the butter, cube by cube, stirring constantly until it has all been incorporated. Season to taste with pepper and serve warm with the asparagus.

GRANDMA'S TIP
Fresh asparagus will last for 3–4 days in a refrigerator. Do not wash asparagus before storing. Wash it just before using.

QUICK & SIMPLE FIX

Bubble & Squeak

SERVES 2–3

INGREDIENTS

- 450 g/1 lb green cabbage
- 4 tbsp olive oil
- 1 onion, thinly sliced
- salt and pepper

MASHED POTATO

- 450 g/1 lb floury potatoes, such as King Edward, Maris Piper or Desirée, peeled and cut into chunks
- 55 g/2 oz butter
- 3 tbsp hot milk
- salt and pepper

1 To make the mashed potato, bring a large saucepan of lightly salted water to the boil, add the potatoes, bring back to the boil and cook for 15–20 minutes, until tender. Drain well and mash with a potato masher until smooth. Season to taste with salt and pepper, add the butter and milk and stir well.

2 Cut the cabbage into quarters, remove the centre stalk and finely shred the leaves.

3 Add half the oil to a large frying pan, then add the onion and fry until softened. Add the cabbage to the pan and stir-fry for 2–3 minutes, until softened. Season to taste with salt and pepper, add the mashed potato and mix together well.

4 Press the mixture firmly into the pan and cook over a high heat for 4–5 minutes until the base is crispy. Place a plate over the pan and invert the pan so that the potato cake falls onto the plate. Add the remaining oil to the pan and heat, then slip the cake back into the pan with the uncooked side down.

5 Cook for a further 5 minutes until the base is crispy too. Turn out onto a hot plate and cut into wedges for serving. Serve immediately.

GRANDMA'S TIP
This is a great way to use up leftovers, especially after a big festive dinner. Chopped Brussels sprouts can be substituted for the cabbage.

Hush Puppies

MAKES 30–35 HUSH PUPPIES
INGREDIENTS

- 280 g/10 oz polenta
- 70 g/2½ oz plain flour, sifted
- 1 small onion,
  finely chopped
- 1 tbsp caster sugar
- 2 tsp baking powder
- ½ tsp salt
- 175 ml/6 fl oz milk
- 1 egg, beaten
- corn oil, for deep-frying

1 Stir the polenta, flour, onion, sugar, baking powder and salt together in a bowl and make a well in the centre.

2 Beat the milk and egg together in a jug, then pour into the dry ingredients and stir until a thick batter forms.

3 Heat at least 5 cm/ 2 inches of oil in a deep frying pan or saucepan over a high heat, until the temperature reaches 180°C/350°F, or until a cube of bread browns in 30 seconds.

4 Drop in as many teaspoonfuls of the batter as will fit without overcrowding the frying pan and cook, stirring constantly, until the hush puppies puff up and turn golden.

5 Remove from the oil with a slotted spoon and drain on kitchen paper. Reheat the oil, if necessary, and cook the remaining batter. Serve hot.

GRANDMA'S TIP
Variations of the hush puppies can be made by adding cheese or vegetables to the batter before frying.

Rice & Peas

SERVES 4

INGREDIENTS

- 2 tbsp olive oil
- 1 onion, sliced
- 1 garlic clove, crushed
- 1 tbsp chopped thyme
- 400 ml/14 fl oz vegetable stock
- 200 g/7 oz basmati rice
- 4 tbsp coconut milk
- 400 g/14 oz canned red kidney beans, drained
- salt and pepper
- fresh thyme sprigs, to garnish

1 Heat the oil in a large saucepan, add the onion and fry over a medium heat, stirring, for about 5 minutes until soft.

2 Add the garlic and thyme and stir-fry for 30 seconds.

3 Stir the stock into the pan and bring to the boil.

4 Stir in the rice, then reduce the heat, cover and simmer for 12–15 minutes, until the rice is just tender.

5 Stir in the coconut milk and beans, then season to taste with salt and pepper.

6 Cook gently for 2–3 minutes, stirring occasionally, until thoroughly heated.

7 Serve hot, garnished with thyme.

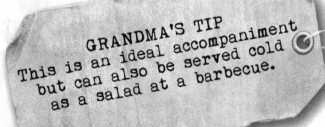

GRANDMA'S TIP
This is an ideal accompaniment but can also be served cold as a salad at a barbecue.

Dauphinoise Potatoes

SERVES 8

INGREDIENTS

- 15 g/½ oz butter, plus extra for greasing
- 1 tbsp plain flour
- 225 ml/8 fl oz double cream
- 450 ml/16 fl oz milk
- 1 tsp salt
- pinch of freshly grated nutmeg
- pinch of freshly ground white pepper
- 4 fresh thyme sprigs
- 2 garlic cloves, finely chopped
- 2 kg/4 lb 8 oz baking potatoes, thinly sliced
- 115 g/4 oz Gruyère cheese or white Cheddar cheese, grated
- salt and pepper

1 Preheat the oven to 190°C/375°F/Gas Mark 5. Grease a 38 × 25-cm/ 15 × 10-inch ovenproof dish.

2 Melt the butter in a saucepan over a medium heat. Stir in the flour and cook, stirring constantly, for 2 minutes. Gradually whisk in the cream and milk and bring to simmering point. Add the salt, the nutmeg, white pepper, thyme and garlic, reduce the heat to low and simmer for 5 minutes. Remove the thyme sprigs.

3 Make a layer of half the potatoes in the prepared dish and season generously with salt and pepper. Top with half the sauce and cover with half the cheese. Repeat the layers with the remaining potatoes, sauce and cheese.

4 Bake in the preheated oven for about 1 hour, or until the top is browned and the potatoes are tender. Remove from the oven and leave to rest for 15 minutes before serving.

GRANDMA'S TIP
These creamy, garlicky potatoes make the perfect side dish for any Sunday roast.

Roast Vegetables

SERVES 4–6

INGREDIENTS

- 3 parsnips, cut into
  5-cm/2-inch chunks
- 4 baby turnips,
  cut into quarters
- 3 carrots, cut into
  5-cm/2-inch chunks
- 450 g/1 lb butternut squash,
  peeled and cut into
  5-cm/2-inch chunks
- 450 g/1 lb sweet potatoes,
  peeled and cut into
  5-cm/2-inch chunks
- 2 garlic cloves,
  finely chopped
- 2 tbsp chopped
  fresh rosemary
- 2 tbsp chopped fresh thyme
- 2 tsp chopped fresh sage
- 3 tbsp olive oil
- salt and pepper
- 2 tbsp chopped fresh mixed
  herbs, such as parsley, thyme
  and mint, to garnish

1 Preheat the oven to 220°C/425°F/Gas Mark 7.

2 Arrange all the vegetables in a single layer in a large roasting tin. Scatter over the garlic and the herbs. Pour over the oil and season well with salt and pepper.

3 Toss all the ingredients together until they are well mixed and coated with the oil (you can leave them to marinate at this stage to allow the flavours to be absorbed).

4 Roast the vegetables at the top of the oven for 50–60 minutes until they are cooked and nicely browned. Turn the vegetables over halfway through the cooking time.

5 Serve with a good handful of fresh herbs scattered on top and a final sprinkling of salt and pepper to taste.

DELICIOUS & ECONOMICAL

Courgette Fritters

MAKES 20–30 FRITTERS

INGREDIENTS

- 100 g/3½ oz
  self–raising flour
- 2 eggs, beaten
- 50 ml/2 fl oz milk
- 300 g/10½ oz courgettes
- 2 tbsp fresh thyme,
  plus extra to garnish
- 1 tbsp oil
- salt and pepper

1 Sift the flour into a large bowl and make a well in the centre. Add the eggs to the well and, using a wooden spoon, gradually draw in the flour.

2 Slowly add the milk to the mixture, stirring constantly to form a thick batter.

3 Meanwhile, grate the courgettes over a sheet of kitchen paper placed in a bowl to absorb some of the juices.

4 Add the courgettes, thyme and salt and pepper, to taste, to the batter and mix thoroughly, for about a minute.

5 Heat the oil in a large, heavy-based frying pan. Taking a tablespoon of the batter for a medium-sized fritter or half a tablespoon of batter for a smaller-sized fritter, spoon the mixture into the hot oil and cook, in batches, for 3–4 minutes on each side.

6 Remove the fritters with a slotted spoon and drain thoroughly on absorbent kitchen paper. Keep each batch warm in the oven while making the rest. Transfer to serving plates and garnish with the thyme.

Coleslaw

SERVES 10–12

INGREDIENTS

- 150 ml/5 fl oz mayonnaise
- 150 ml/5 fl oz natural yogurt
- dash of Tabasco sauce
- 1 head of white cabbage
- 4 carrots
- 1 green pepper
- salt and pepper

1 Mix the mayonnaise, yogurt, Tabasco sauce, and salt and pepper to taste together in a small bowl. Chill in the refrigerator until required.

2 Cut the cabbage in half and then into quarters. Remove and discard the tough centre stalk. Finely shred the cabbage leaves. Wash the leaves under cold running water and dry thoroughly on kitchen paper. Roughly grate the carrots or shred in a food processor or on a mandoline. Finely chop the green pepper.

3 Mix the vegetables together in a large serving bowl and toss to mix. Pour over the dressing and toss until the vegetables are well coated. Cover and chill in the refrigerator until required.

GRANDMA'S TIP
You can add in plenty of other ingredients to add taste, colour and texture, such as smoked almonds, capers, apples, toasted pecan nuts, sunflower seeds and pumpkin seeds.

Red Wine Sauce

MAKES ABOUT
225 ML/8 FL OZ
INGREDIENTS

- 150 ml/5 fl oz Gravy
  (see page 137)
- 4 tbsp red wine,
  such as a Burgundy
- 1 tbsp redcurrant jelly

1 Blend the gravy with the wine and pour into a small, heavy-based saucepan. Add the redcurrant jelly and warm over a gentle heat, stirring, until blended.

2 Bring to the boil, then reduce the heat and simmer for 2 minutes. Serve hot.

GRANDMA'S TIP
For a richer sauce, ideal as an accompaniment to game dishes, replace half the red wine with Marsala, sherry or port.

Gravy

MAKES ABOUT
1.2 LITRES/2 PINTS
INGREDIENTS

- 900 g/2 lb meat bones, raw or cooked
- 1 large onion, chopped
- 1 large carrot, chopped
- 2 celery sticks, chopped
- 1 bouquet garni
- 1.7 litres/3 pints water

1 Preheat the oven to 200°C/400°F/ Gas Mark 6. Put the bones in a roasting tin and roast in the preheated oven for 20 minutes, or until browned. Remove from the oven and leave to cool.

2 Chop the bones into small pieces and put in a large saucepan with all the remaining ingredients. Bring to the boil, then reduce the heat, cover and simmer for 2 hours.

3 Strain and leave until cold, then remove all traces of fat. Store, covered, in the refrigerator for up to 4 days. Boil vigorously for 5 minutes before using. The gravy can be frozen in ice-cube trays for up to 1 month.

Mint & Spinach Chutney

SERVES 4–6

INGREDIENTS

- 55 g/2 oz tender fresh
  spinach leaves
- 3 tbsp fresh mint leaves
- 2 tbsp chopped fresh
  coriander leaves
- 1 small red onion,
  coarsely chopped
- 1 small garlic clove, chopped
- 1 fresh green chilli, chopped
  (deseeded, if liked)
- 2½ tsp sugar
- 1 tbsp tamarind juice or juice
  of ½ lemon

1 Place all the ingredients in a food processor and process until smooth, adding only as much water as is necessary to enable the blades to move.

2 Transfer to a serving bowl, cover and leave to chill in the refrigerator for at least 30 minutes before serving. Serve with samosas or lamb kebabs.

GRANDMA'S TIP
For an even cooler chutney to serve with very spicy dishes, omit the spinach, double the quantity of coriander and be sure to deseed the chilli.

Bread Sauce

SERVES 6–9

INGREDIENTS

- 1 onion
- 12 cloves
- 1 bay leaf
- 6 black peppercorns
- 600 ml/1 pint milk
- 115 g/4 oz fresh white breadcrumbs
- 2 tbsp butter
- whole nutmeg, for grating
- 2 tbsp double cream (optional)
- salt and pepper

1 Make small holes in the onion using the point of a sharp knife or a skewer, then stick a clove in each hole.

2 Put the onion, bay leaf and peppercorns in a saucepan and pour in the milk. Bring to the boil over a medium heat, then remove from the heat, cover and leave to infuse for 1 hour.

3 To make the sauce, discard the onion and bay leaf and strain the milk to remove the peppercorns. Return the milk to the cleaned pan and add the breadcrumbs.

4 Cook over a very low heat for 4–5 minutes, until the breadcrumbs have swollen and the sauce is thick.

5 Beat in the butter and season well with salt and pepper and a good grating of nutmeg. Stir in the cream just before serving, if using.

Corn Relish

MAKES ABOUT
600 G/1 LB 5 OZ
INGREDIENTS

- 5 corn cobs,
  about 900 g/2 lb, husked
- 1 red pepper, deseeded and
  finely diced
- 2 celery sticks,
  very finely chopped
- 1 red onion, finely chopped
- 125 g/4½ oz sugar
- 1 tbsp salt
- 2 tbsp mustard powder
- ½ tsp celery seeds
- small pinch of
  turmeric (optional)
- 225 ml/8 fl oz cider vinegar
- 125 ml/4 fl oz water

1 Bring a large saucepan of lightly salted water to the boil and fill a bowl with iced water. Add the corn to the boiling water, return the water to the boil and boil for 2 minutes, or until the kernels are tender-crisp. Using tongs, immediately plunge the cobs into the cold water to halt cooking. Remove from the water and cut the kernels from the cobs, then set aside.

2 Add the red pepper, celery and onion to the corn cooking water, bring back to the boil and boil for 2 minutes, or until tender-crisp. Drain well and return to the pan with the corn kernels.

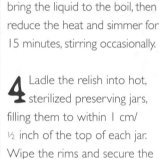

3 Put the sugar, salt, mustard, celery seeds and turmeric, if using, into a bowl and mix together, then stir in the vinegar and water. Add to the pan, bring the liquid to the boil, then reduce the heat and simmer for 15 minutes, stirring occasionally.

4 Ladle the relish into hot, sterilized preserving jars, filling them to within 1 cm/ ½ inch of the top of each jar. Wipe the rims and secure the lids. Leave the relish to cool completely, then refrigerate for up to 2 months.

PRACTICE MAKES PERFECT

White Chocolate Fudge Sauce

SERVES 4

INGREDIENTS

- 150 ml/5 fl oz double cream
- 4 tbsp unsalted butter,
  cut into small pieces
- 3 tbsp caster sugar
- 175 g/6 oz white chocolate,
  broken into pieces
- 2 tbsp brandy

1 Pour the cream into the top of a double boiler or a heatproof bowl set over a saucepan of gently simmering water. Add the butter and sugar and stir until the mixture is smooth. Remove from the heat.

2 Stir in the chocolate, a few pieces at a time, waiting until each batch has melted before adding the next. Add the brandy and stir the sauce until smooth. Cool to room temperature before serving.

GRANDMA'S TIP
You can give this sauce a citrussy zing by replacing the brandy with the same quantity of an orange liqueur, such as Cointreau or Grand Marnier.

Chocolate Brandy Sauce

SERVES 4
INGREDIENTS

- 250 g/9 oz plain chocolate (must contain at least 50 per cent cocoa solids)
- 100 ml/3½ fl oz double cream
- 2 tbsp brandy

1 Break or chop the chocolate into small pieces and place in the top of a double boiler or in a heatproof bowl set over a saucepan of simmering water.

2 Pour in the cream and stir until melted and smooth. Stir in the brandy, pour into a jug and serve.

IMPRESS THE FAMILY

Home-made Vanilla Custard

SERVES 4–6

INGREDIENTS

- 300 ml / 10 fl oz milk
- 2 eggs
- 2 tsp caster sugar
- 1 vanilla pod, split, or 1 tsp vanilla extract

1 Put 2 tablespoons of the milk, the eggs and sugar into a heatproof bowl that will fit over a saucepan of simmering water without the bottom of the bowl touching the water, then set aside.

2 Put the remaining milk into a small, heavy-based saucepan over a medium–high heat and heat just until small bubbles appear around the edge. Scrape half the vanilla seeds into the milk and add the pod. Remove the pan from the heat, cover and leave to infuse for 30 minutes.

3 Bring a kettle of water to the boil. Meanwhile, using an electric mixer, beat the milk, eggs and sugar until pale and thick. Slowly beat in the warm milk.

4 Pour a thin layer of boiling water into a saucepan, place over a low heat and fit the bowl containing the milk mixture snugly on top. Cook, stirring constantly, for 10–15 minutes, until the sauce becomes thick enough to hold the impression of your finger if you rub it along the back of the spoon. It is important that the bottom of the bowl never touches the water and that the sauce doesn't boil. If the sauce looks as if it is about to boil, remove the bowl from the pan and continue stirring.

5 Strain the hot custard into a separate bowl. If you have not used a vanilla pod and seeds stir in the vanilla extract. The custard can be used immediately, or left to cool completely, then covered and chilled for up to one day. The sauce will thicken on cooling.

GRANDMA'S TIP
Keep the used vanilla pod in a jar of caster sugar and use the flavoured sugar for making cakes, sprinkling over fruit or making dessert sauces.

GRANDMA'S
BAKING DAY

Pineapple Upside-down Cake

SERVES 10

INGREDIENTS

- 4 eggs, beaten
- 200 g/7 oz golden caster sugar
- 1 tsp vanilla extract
- 200 g/7 oz plain flour
- 2 tsp baking powder
- 125 g/4½ oz unsalted butter, melted, plus extra for greasing

TOPPING

- 40 g/1½ oz unsalted butter
- 4 tbsp golden syrup
- 425 g/15 oz canned pineapple rings, drained
- 4–6 glacé cherries, halved

1 Preheat the oven to 160°C/325°F/Gas Mark 3. Grease a 23-cm/9-inch round deep tin with a solid base and line the base with baking paper.

2 To make the topping, place the butter and golden syrup in a heavy-based saucepan and heat gently until melted. Bring to the boil and boil for 2–3 minutes, stirring, until slightly thickened and toffee-like.

3 Pour the syrup into the base of the prepared tin. Arrange the pineapple rings and glacé cherries in one layer over the syrup.

4 Place the eggs, sugar and vanilla extract in a large heatproof bowl over a saucepan of gently simmering water and whisk with an electric mixer for about 10–15 minutes, until thick enough to leave a trail when the whisk is lifted. Sift in the flour and baking powder and fold in lightly and evenly with a metal spoon.

5 Fold the melted butter into the mixture with a metal spoon until evenly mixed. Spoon into the prepared tin and bake in the preheated oven for 1–1¼ hours, or until well risen, firm and golden brown.

6 Leave to cool in the tin for 10 minutes, then carefully turn out onto a serving plate. Serve warm or cold.

GRANDMA'S TIP

If your cake sinks in the middle, cut it out to make a ring cake, spread with whipped cream and fill the centre with fresh berries.

Victoria Sponge Cake

SERVES 8–10

INGREDIENTS

- 175 g/6 oz butter, at room temperature, plus extra for greasing
- 175 g/6 oz caster sugar
- 3 eggs, beaten
- 175 g/6 oz self-raising flour
- pinch of salt
- raspberry jam
- double cream, whipped
- 1 tbsp caster sugar or icing sugar, for dusting

1 Preheat the oven to 180°C/350°F/Gas Mark 4.

2 Grease two 20-cm/8-inch sponge tins and line with greaseproof paper or baking paper.

3 Cream the butter and sugar together in a mixing bowl using a wooden spoon or a hand-held mixer until the mixture is pale in colour and light and fluffy.

4 Add the eggs a little at a time, beating well after each addition.

5 Sift the flour and salt together and carefully add to the mixture, folding in with a metal spoon or a spatula. Divide the mixture between the tins and smooth over with the spatula.

6 Place them on the same shelf in the centre of the preheated oven and bake for 25–30 minutes until well risen, golden brown and beginning to shrink from the sides of the tins.

7 Remove from the oven and leave to stand for 1 minute.

8 Loosen the cakes from around the edges of the tins using a palette knife. Turn the cakes out onto a clean tea towel, remove the paper and invert them onto a wire rack (this prevents the wire rack marking the tops of the cakes).

9 When completely cool, sandwich together with the jam and cream and sprinkle with icing sugar.

FEEL-BETTER FOOD

Blueberry Crumb Cake

SERVES 12

INGREDIENTS

- 280 g/10 oz fresh blueberries
- 450 g/1 lb self-raising flour, plus extra for dusting
- 1¼ tsp salt
- ½ tsp mixed spice
- 280 g/10 oz butter, at room temperature, plus extra for greasing
- 350 g/12 oz caster sugar
- ½ tsp vanilla extract
- ½ tsp almond extract
- 2 large eggs
- 300–350 ml/10–12 fl oz soured cream

- CRUMB TOPPING
- 115 g/4 oz butter, diced
- 140 g/5 oz plain flour
- 2 tbsp soft light brown sugar
- 1 tbsp granulated sugar
- 85 g/3 oz almonds, chopped

1 To make the crumb topping, put the butter and flour into a large bowl and rub together until the mixture resembles coarse breadcrumbs. Stir in both types of sugar and the almonds, then leave to chill in the refrigerator until required.

2 Preheat the oven to 180°C/350°F/Gas Mark 4. Grease a 33 x 23-cm/ 13 x 9-inch rectangular cake tin and dust with flour. Dust the blueberries with 1 tablespoon of the measured flour and set aside. Sift the remaining flour into a bowl with the salt and mixed spice and set aside.

3 Place the butter in a large bowl and, using an electric mixer, beat until soft and creamy. Add the sugar, vanilla extract and almond extract and continue beating until the

mixture is light and fluffy. Add the eggs, one at a time, beating well after each addition, then beat in 300 ml/10 fl oz of the soured cream. Beat in the flour until the mixture is soft and falls easily from a spoon. Add the remaining soured cream, 1 tablespoon at a time, if necessary.

4 Add the blueberries and any loose flour to the batter and quickly fold in. Pour the batter into the prepared tin and smooth the surface. Pinch the topping into large crumbs and scatter evenly over the batter.

5 Bake the cake in the preheated oven for 45–55 minutes until it comes away from the side of the tin and a cocktail stick inserted into the centre comes out clean. Transfer the tin to a wire rack and leave to cool completely. Cut the cake into 12 slices and serve straight from the tin.

GRANDMA'S TIP
When a recipe says 'dot with butter', shave off curls from a cold block with a vegetable peeler.

Angel Food Cake

SERVES 10

INGREDIENTS

- sunflower oil, for greasing
- 8 large egg whites
- 1 tsp cream of tartar
- 1 tsp almond extract
- 250 g/9 oz caster sugar
- 115 g/4 oz plain flour, plus extra for dusting

TO SERVE
- 250 g/9 oz summer berries
- 1 tbsp lemon juice
- 2 tbsp icing sugar

1 Preheat the oven to 160°C/325°F/Gas Mark 3. Brush the inside of a 1.7-litre/3-pint ring tin with oil and dust lightly with flour.

2 Whisk the egg whites in a clean, grease-free bowl until they hold soft peaks. Add the cream of tartar and whisk again until the whites are stiff but not dry.

3 Whisk in the almond extract, then add the sugar, a tablespoon at a time, whisking hard between each addition. Sift in the flour and fold in lightly and evenly, using a large metal spoon.

4 Spoon the mixture into the prepared cake tin and tap on the work surface to remove any large air bubbles. Bake in the preheated oven for 40–45 minutes, or until golden brown and firm to the touch.

5 Run the tip of a small knife around the edges of the cake to loosen it from the tin. Leave to cool in the tin for 10 minutes, then turn out onto a wire rack to finish cooling.

6 To serve, place the berries, lemon juice and icing sugar in a saucepan and heat gently until the sugar has dissolved. Serve with the cake.

GRANDMA'S TIP
The delicious Angel Food Cake takes its name from its light and airy white sponge.

Devil's Food Cake

SERVES 8–10
INGREDIENTS

- 140 g/5 oz plain chocolate
- 100 ml/3½ fl oz milk
- 2 tbsp cocoa powder
- 140 g/5 oz unsalted butter, plus extra for greasing
- 140 g/5 oz light muscovado sugar
- 3 eggs, separated
- 4 tbsp soured cream or crème fraîche
- 200 g/7 oz plain flour
- 1 tsp bicarbonate of soda

FROSTING

- 140 g/5 oz plain chocolate
- 40 g/1½ oz cocoa powder
- 4 tbsp soured cream or crème fraîche
- 1 tbsp golden syrup
- 40 g/1½ oz unsalted butter
- 4 tbsp water
- 200 g/7 oz icing sugar

1 Preheat the oven to 160°C/325°F/Gas Mark 3. Grease two 20-cm/8-inch sandwich tins and line the bases with non-stick baking paper.

2 Break up the chocolate and place in a heatproof bowl over a saucepan of simmering water, add the milk and cocoa powder, then heat gently, stirring, until melted and smooth. Remove from the heat.

3 In a large bowl beat the butter and muscovado sugar together until pale and fluffy. Beat in the egg yolks, then beat in the soured cream and the melted chocolate mixture.

4 Sift in the flour and bicarbonate of soda, then fold in evenly. In a separate bowl, whisk the egg whites until stiff enough to hold firm peaks. Fold into the mixture lightly and evenly.

5 Divide the mixture between the prepared cake tins, smooth level and bake in the preheated oven for 35–40 minutes, or until risen and firm to the touch. Cool in the tins for 10 minutes, then turn out onto a wire rack.

6 To make the frosting, put the chocolate, cocoa powder, soured cream, golden syrup, butter and water in a saucepan and heat gently, until melted. Remove from the heat and sift in the sugar, stirring until smooth. Cool, stirring occasionally, until the mixture begins to thicken and hold its shape.

7 Split the cakes in half horizontally with a sharp knife, to make four layers. Sandwich the cakes together with about a third of the frosting. Spread the remainder over the top and side of the cake, swirling with a palette knife.

GRANDMA'S TIP
Use a metal, ceramic or glass bowl when whisking egg whites. Plastic bowls scratch easily, so may not be grease-free, and will prevent the whites foaming.

Lemon Drizzle Cake

SERVES 8

INGREDIENTS

- butter, for greasing
- 200 g/7 oz plain flour
- 2 tsp baking powder
- 200 g/7 oz caster sugar
- 4 eggs
- 150 ml/5 fl oz soured cream
- grated rind of 1 large lemon
- 4 tbsp lemon juice
- 150 ml/5 fl oz sunflower oil

SYRUP

- 4 tbsp icing sugar
- 3 tbsp lemon juice

1 Preheat the oven to 180°C/350°F/Gas Mark 4. Lightly grease a 20-cm/8-inch loose-based round cake tin and line the base with baking paper.

2 Sift the flour and baking powder together into a mixing bowl and stir in the sugar.

3 In a separate bowl, whisk the eggs, soured cream, lemon rind, lemon juice and oil together.

4 Pour the egg mixture into the dry ingredients and mix well until evenly combined.

5 Pour the mixture into the prepared tin and bake in the preheated oven for 45–60 minutes, until risen and golden brown.

6 Meanwhile, to make the syrup, mix the icing sugar and lemon juice together in a small saucepan. Stir over a low heat until just beginning to bubble and turn syrupy.

7 As soon as the cake comes out of the oven, prick the surface with a fine skewer, then brush the syrup over the top. Leave the cake to cool completely in the tin before turning out and serving.

GRANDMA'S GUILTY PLEASURE

Apple Streusel Cake

SERVES 8

INGREDIENTS

- 450 g/1 lb cooking apples
- 175 g/6 oz self-raising flour
- 1 tsp ground cinnamon
- pinch of salt
- 115 g/4 oz butter, plus extra for greasing
- 115 g/4 oz caster sugar
- 2 eggs
- 1–2 tbsp milk
- icing sugar, for dusting

STREUSEL TOPPING

- 115 g/4 oz self-raising flour
- 85 g/3 oz butter
- 85 g/3 oz caster sugar

1 Preheat the oven to 180°C/350°F/Gas Mark 4, then grease a 23-cm/9-inch springform cake tin. To make the streusel topping, sift the flour into a bowl and rub in the butter until the mixture resembles coarse crumbs. Stir in the sugar and reserve.

2 To make the cake, peel, core and thinly slice the apples. Sift the flour into a bowl with the cinnamon and salt. Place the butter and sugar in a separate bowl and beat together until light and fluffy. Gradually beat in the eggs, adding a little of the flour mixture with the last addition of egg. Gently fold in half the remaining flour mixture, then fold in the rest with the milk.

3 Spoon the mixture into the prepared tin and smooth the top. Cover with the sliced apples and sprinkle the streusel topping evenly over the top.

4 Bake in the preheated oven for 1 hour, or until browned and firm to the touch. Leave to cool in the tin before opening the sides. Dust the cake with icing sugar before serving.

FEEL-BETTER FOOD

Millionaires' Shortbread

MAKES 12 SLICES

INGREDIENTS

• 115 g/4 oz butter, plus extra for greasing
• 175 g/6 oz plain flour
• 55 g/2 oz golden caster sugar
• 200 g/7 oz plain chocolate, broken into pieces

FILLING

• 175 g/6 oz butter
• 115 g/4 oz golden caster sugar
• 3 tbsp golden syrup
• 400 ml/14 fl oz canned condensed milk

1 Preheat the oven to 180°C/350°F/Gas Mark 4. Grease and line the base of a 23-cm/9-inch shallow, square cake tin.

2 Place the butter, flour and sugar in a food processor and process until the mixture begins to bind together. Press it into the prepared tin and smooth the top. Bake in the preheated oven for 20–25 minutes, or until golden.

3 Meanwhile, make the filling. Place the butter, sugar, golden syrup and condensed milk in a saucepan and heat gently over a low heat until the sugar is dissolved.

4 Bring to the boil and simmer for 6–8 minutes, stirring constantly, until the mixture becomes very thick. Pour over the shortbread base and leave to chill in the refrigerator until firm.

5 Place the chocolate in a heatproof bowl set over a saucepan of gently simmering water and stir until melted. Leave to cool slightly, then spread over the caramel. Chill in the refrigerator until set. Cut the shortbread into 12 pieces with a sharp knife and serve.

GRANDMA'S TIP
Millionaires' Shortbread, also known as Caramel Shortbread or Caramel Slices, is thought to be of Scottish origin.

Black & White Cookies

MAKES 20 COOKIES
INGREDIENTS

- 115 g/4 oz unsalted butter, plus extra for greasing
- 1 tsp vanilla extract
- 175 g/6 oz caster sugar
- 2 eggs, beaten
- 300 g/10½ oz plain flour
- ½ tsp baking powder
- 200 ml/7 fl oz milk

ICING

- 225 g/8 oz icing sugar
- 125 ml/4 fl oz double cream
- ⅛ tsp vanilla extract
- 75 g/2¾ oz plain chocolate, broken into pieces

1 Preheat the oven to 190°C/375°F/Gas Mark 5. Grease three baking sheets. Place the butter, vanilla extract and caster sugar in a large bowl. Beat the mixture with a whisk until light and fluffy and then beat in the eggs one at a time.

2 Sift the flour and baking powder and fold into the creamed mixture, loosening with milk as you go until both are used up and the mixture is of dropping consistency.

3 Drop heaped tablespoonfuls of the mixture, spaced well apart, on the prepared baking sheets. Place in the preheated oven and bake for 15 minutes until turning golden at the edges and light to the touch. Transfer to wire racks to cool completely.

4 To make the icing, put the icing sugar in a bowl and mix in half the cream and the vanilla extract. The consistency should be thick but spreadable.

Using a palette knife, spread half of each cookie with white icing. Now, melt the chocolate in a heatproof bowl over a pan of simmering water. The base of the bowl should not touch the water. Remove from the heat and stir in the remaining cream. Spread the dark icing over the uncoated cookie halves.

Chocolate Chip Cookies

MAKES 30 COOKIES
INGREDIENTS

- 175 g/6 oz plain flour
- 1 tsp baking powder
- 125 g/4½ oz soft margarine,
  plus extra for greasing
- 85 g/3 oz light muscovado
  sugar
- 55 g/2 oz caster sugar
- ½ tsp vanilla extract
- 1 egg
- 125 g/4½ oz plain chocolate
  chips

1 Preheat the oven to 190°C/375°F/Gas Mark 5. Lightly grease two baking trays.

2 Place all of the ingredients in a large mixing bowl and beat until well combined.

3 Place tablespoonfuls of the mixture on the prepared baking trays, spacing them well apart to allow for spreading during cooking.

4 Bake in the preheated oven for 10–12 minutes, or until the cookies are golden brown. Using a palette knife, transfer the cookies to a wire rack to cool completely.

5 Serve immediately or store in an airtight container.

Chocolate Brownies

MAKES 16 SQUARES

INGREDIENTS

- groundnut oil, for greasing
- 225 g/8 oz good-quality plain chocolate, at least 60 per cent cocoa solids
- 175 g/6 oz butter
- 3 large eggs
- 100 g/3½ oz caster sugar
- 175 g/6 oz self-raising flour
- 100 g/3½ oz walnuts or blanched hazelnuts, chopped
- 50 g/1¾ oz milk chocolate chips

1 Preheat the oven to 180°C/350°F/Gas Mark 4. Lightly grease a 25-cm/10-inch square non-stick, shallow baking tin.

2 Break the chocolate into a heatproof bowl and place over a small saucepan of simmering water. It is important that the base of the bowl doesn't touch the water.

3 Add the butter to the chocolate, set the bowl over the saucepan and heat the water to a slow simmer. Leave the chocolate, undisturbed, to melt very slowly – this will take about 10 minutes. Remove the bowl from the pan and stir well to combine the chocolate and the butter.

4 Meanwhile, beat the eggs and sugar together in a bowl until pale cream in colour. Stir in the melted chocolate mixture, then add the flour, nuts and chocolate chips. Mix everything together well.

5 Tip the mixture into the prepared baking tin and bake in the preheated oven for 30 minutes, or until the top is set – if the centre is still slightly sticky, that will be all the better. Leave to cool in the tin, then lift out and cut into squares.

CHILDREN'S FAVOURITE

Vanilla-frosted Cupcakes

MAKES 12 CUPCAKES
INGREDIENTS

- 115 g/4 oz butter, softened
- 115 g/4 oz caster sugar
- 2 eggs, lightly beaten
- 115 g/4 oz self-raising flour
- 1 tbsp milk
- 1 tbsp coloured sprinkles

FROSTING

- 175 g/6 oz unsalted butter, softened
- 1 tsp vanilla extract
- 280 g/10 oz icing sugar, sifted

1 Preheat the oven to 180°C/350°F/Gas Mark 4. Put 12 paper baking cases in a bun tray or put 12 double-layer paper cases on a baking tray.

2 Put the butter and sugar in a bowl. Beat together until light and fluffy.

3 Gradually beat in the eggs. Sift in the flour and fold in with the milk.

4 Spoon the mixture into the paper cases. Bake in the preheated oven for 20 minutes until golden brown and firm to the touch. Transfer to a wire rack to cool.

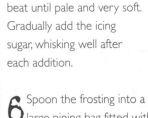

5 To make the frosting, put the butter and vanilla extract in a bowl and beat until pale and very soft. Gradually add the icing sugar, whisking well after each addition.

6 Spoon the frosting into a large piping bag fitted with a medium star-shaped nozzle and pipe swirls of frosting on the top of each cupcake.

7 Serve decorated with sprinkles.

GRANDMA'S TIP
To make mini versions of these cupcakes, divide the mixture between 30 mini cupcake cases and reduce the cooking time to 8-10 minutes.

Raisin Bran Muffins

MAKES 12 MUFFINS
INGREDIENTS

- 140 g/5 oz plain flour
- 1 tbsp baking powder
- 140 g/5 oz wheat bran
- 115 g/4 oz caster sugar
- 150 g/5½ oz raisins
- 2 eggs
- 250 ml/9 fl oz skimmed milk
- 90 ml/ 6 tbsp sunflower oil, plus extra for greasing
- 1 tsp vanilla extract

1 Preheat the oven to 200°C/400°F/Gas Mark 6. Grease a 12-cup muffin tin or line with 12 paper cases. Sift the flour and baking powder together into a large bowl. Stir in the bran, sugar and raisins.

2 Lightly beat the eggs in a large jug or bowl, then beat in the milk, oil and vanilla extract. Make a well in the centre of the dry ingredients and pour in the beaten liquid ingredients. Stir gently until just combined; do not over-mix.

3 Spoon the mixture into the prepared muffin tin. Bake in the preheated oven for about 20 minutes, until well risen, golden brown and firm to the touch.

4 Leave the muffins in the tin for 5 minutes then serve warm or transfer to a wire rack and leave to cool.

Cinnamon Swirls

MAKES 12 SWIRLS
INGREDIENTS

- 225 g/8 oz strong white flour
- ½ tsp salt
- 10 g/¼ oz easy-blend dried yeast
- 2 tbsp butter, cut into small pieces, plus extra for greasing
- 1 egg, lightly beaten
- 125 ml/4 fl oz lukewarm milk
- 2 tbsp maple syrup, for glazing

FILLING
- 4 tbsp butter, softened
- 2 tsp ground cinnamon
- 50 g/1¾ oz soft light brown sugar
- 50 g/1¾ oz currants

1 Grease a baking sheet with a little butter.

2 Sift the flour and salt into a mixing bowl. Stir in the yeast. Rub in the butter with your fingertips until the mixture resembles breadcrumbs. Add the egg and milk and mix to form a dough.

3 Form the dough into a ball, place in a greased bowl, cover and leave to stand in a warm place for about 40 minutes, or until doubled in size.

4 Lightly knock back the dough for 1 minute, then roll out to a rectangle measuring 30 × 23 cm/ 12 × 9 inches.

5 To make the filling, cream together the butter, cinnamon and sugar until light and fluffy. Spread the filling evenly over the dough rectangle, leaving a 2.5-cm/ 1-inch border all around. Sprinkle the currants evenly over the top.

6 Roll up the dough from one of the long edges, and press down to seal. Cut the roll into 12 slices. Place them, cut-side down, on the baking sheet, cover and leave to stand for 30 minutes.

7 Meanwhile, preheat the oven to 190°C/375°F/ Gas Mark 5. Bake the buns in the preheated oven for 20–30 minutes, or until well risen. Brush with the maple syrup and leave to cool slightly before serving.

Salted Caramel Pies

SERVES 6

INGREDIENTS

CRUMB CRUST
- 175 g/6 oz digestive biscuits, finely crushed
- 85 g/3 oz butter, melted

FILLING
- 300 g/10½ oz caster sugar
- 150 g/5½ oz butter
- ¼ tsp sea salt crystals
- 125 ml/4 fl oz double cream

TOPPING
- 150 ml/5 fl oz double cream
- chocolate curls or shavings

1 To make the crumb crust, place the crushed biscuits in a bowl and stir in the melted butter. Divide the mixture between four tartlet tins and press down firmly into the base and up the sides of each tin. Chill in the refrigerator for 30 minutes.

2 To make the filling, place the sugar and 4 tablespoons of water into a heavy-based saucepan. Heat gently, stirring, until the sugar has dissolved. Bring the syrup to a boil and boil, without stirring, until the liquid is a golden toffee colour. Remove from the heat and cool for 2 minutes, then carefully stir in the butter and half the salt.

3 Gradually whisk in the cream and continue whisking until the mixture is smooth and glossy. Transfer to a heatproof bowl and leave to cool and thicken, stirring occasionally. Stir in the rest of the salt. Spoon the cooled caramel into the tartlet cases.

4 For the topping, whip the cream until holding soft peaks. Drop large spoonfuls on top of the caramel filling, scatter over the chocolate curls or shavings and serve.

GRANDMA'S TIP
These delicious pies, topped with cream and chocolate shavings, are perfect to serve at a dinner party or as an afternoon treat.

Oat & Potato Bread

MAKES I LOAF

INGREDIENTS

- vegetable oil, for greasing
- 225 g/8 oz peeled floury potatoes
- 500 g/1 lb 2 oz strong white flour, plus extra for dusting
- 1½ tsp salt
- 40 g/1½ oz butter, diced
- 1½ tsp easy-blend dried yeast
- 1½ tbsp soft dark brown sugar
- 3 tbsp rolled oats
- 2 tbsp skimmed milk powder
- 210 ml/7½ fl oz lukewarm water

TOPPING

- 1 tbsp water
- 1 tbsp rolled oats

1 Grease a 900-g/2-lb loaf tin. Put the potatoes in a large saucepan, add water to cover and bring to the boil. Cook for 20–25 minutes, until tender. Drain, then mash until smooth. Leave to cool.

2 Sift the flour and salt together into a warmed bowl. Rub in the butter with your fingertips. Stir in the yeast, sugar, oats and milk powder. Mix in the mashed potato, then add the water and mix to a soft dough.

3 Turn out the dough onto a lightly floured work surface and knead for 5–10 minutes, or until smooth and elastic. Brush a bowl with oil and put the dough into it, cover with clingfilm and leave to rise in a warm place for 1 hour, or until doubled in size.

4 Turn out the dough again and knead lightly. Shape into a loaf and transfer to the prepared tin. Cover and leave to rise in a warm place for 30 minutes. Meanwhile, preheat the oven to 220°C/425°F/Gas Mark 7.

5 To make the topping, brush the surface of the loaf with the water and carefully sprinkle over the oats. Bake in the preheated oven for 25–30 minutes, or until it sounds hollow when tapped on the base. Transfer to a wire rack and leave to cool slightly. Serve warm.

GRANDMA'S TIP
Rather than make mashed potato from scratch, this recipe is a frugal way to make good use of your leftovers.

Sourdough Bread

MAKES 2 LOAVES
INGREDIENTS

- 450 g/1 lb wholemeal flour
- 4 tsp salt
- 350 ml/12 fl oz
  lukewarm water
- 2 tbsp black treacle
- 1 tbsp vegetable oil, plus
  extra for brushing
- plain flour, for dusting

STARTER
- 85 g/3 oz wholemeal flour
- 85 g/3 oz strong
  white flour
- 55 g/2 oz caster sugar
- 250 ml/9 fl oz milk

1 For the starter, put the wholemeal flour, strong white flour, sugar and milk into a non-metallic bowl and beat well with a fork. Cover with a damp tea towel and leave to stand at room temperature for 4–5 days, until the mixture is frothy and smells sour.

2 Sift the flour and half the salt together into a bowl and add the water, treacle, oil and starter. Mix well with a wooden spoon until a dough begins to form, then knead with your hands until it leaves the side of the bowl. Turn out onto a lightly floured surface and knead for 10 minutes, until smooth and elastic.

3 Brush a bowl with oil. Form the dough into a ball, put it into the bowl and put the bowl into a polythene bag or cover with a damp tea towel. Leave to rise in a warm place for 2 hours, until the dough has doubled in volume.

4 Dust two baking sheets with flour. Mix the remaining salt with 4 tablespoons of water in a bowl. Turn out the dough on to a lightly floured work surface and knock back with your fist, then knead for a further 10 minutes. Halve the dough, shape each piece into an oval and place the loaves on the prepared baking sheets. Brush with the saltwater glaze and leave to stand in a warm place, brushing frequently with the glaze, for 30 minutes.

5 Preheat the oven to 220°C/425°F/Gas Mark 7. Brush the loaves with the remaining glaze and bake for 30 minutes, until the crust is golden brown and the loaves sound hollow when tapped on their bases with your knuckles. If it is necessary to cook them for longer, reduce the oven temperature to 190°C/375°F/Gas Mark 5. Transfer to wire racks to cool.

Cornbread

MAKES 1 SMALL LOAF

INGREDIENTS

- vegetable oil, for greasing
- 175 g/6 oz plain flour
- 1 tsp salt
- 4 tsp baking powder
- 1 tsp caster sugar
- 280 g/10 oz polenta
- 115 g/4 oz butter, softened
- 4 eggs
- 250 ml/9 fl oz milk
- 3 tbsp double cream

1 Preheat the oven to 200°C/400°F/ Gas Mark 6. Brush a 20-cm/ 8-inch square cake tin with oil.

2 Sift the flour, salt and baking powder together into a bowl. Add the sugar and polenta and stir to mix. Add the butter and cut into the dry ingredients with a knife, then rub it in with your fingertips until the mixture resembles fine breadcrumbs.

3 Lightly beat the eggs in a bowl with the milk and cream, then stir into the polenta mixture until thoroughly combined.

4 Spoon the mixture into the prepared tin and smooth the surface. Bake in the preheated oven for 30–35 minutes, until a wooden cocktail stick inserted into the centre of the loaf comes out clean. Remove the tin from the oven and leave to cool for 5–10 minutes, then cut into squares and serve warm.

PRACTICE MAKES PERFECT

GRANDMA'S JUST DESSERTS

Banana Cream Pie

SERVES 8–10

INGREDIENTS

- flour, for dusting
- 350 g/12 oz ready-made shortcrust pastry, thawed, if frozen
- 4 large egg yolks
- 85 g/3 oz caster sugar
- 4 tbsp cornflour
- pinch of salt
- 450 ml/16 fl oz milk
- 1 tsp vanilla extract
- 3 bananas
- ½ tbsp lemon juice
- 350 ml/12 fl oz double cream, whipped with 3 tbsp icing sugar, to decorate

1 Preheat the oven to 200°C/400°F/Gas Mark 6. Very lightly flour a rolling pin and use to roll out the pastry on a lightly floured work surface into a 30-cm/12-inch round. Line a 23-cm/9-inch pie plate with the pastry, then trim the excess pastry and prick the base all over with a fork. Line the pastry case with greaseproof paper and fill with baking beans.

2 Bake in the preheated oven for 15 minutes, or until the pastry is a light golden colour. Remove the paper and beans and prick the base again. Return to the oven and bake for a further 5–10 minutes, until golden and dry. Leave to cool completely on a wire rack.

3 Meanwhile, put the egg yolks, sugar, cornflour and salt into a bowl and beat until blended and pale in colour. Beat in the milk and vanilla extract.

4 Pour the mixture into a heavy-based saucepan over a medium–high heat and bring to the boil, stirring, until smooth and thick. Reduce the heat to low and simmer, stirring, for 2 minutes. Strain the mixture into a bowl and set aside to cool.

5 Slice the bananas, place in a bowl with the lemon juice and toss. Arrange them in the cooled pastry case, then top with the custard and chill in the refrigerator for at least 2 hours. Spread the cream over the top of the pie and serve immediately.

GRANDMA'S TIP
Old-fashioned metal pie plates, cake tins and tart tins conduct heat better than glass, earthenware or porcelain, producing even baking and reducing the cooking time.

Lemon Meringue Pie

SERVES 6–8

INGREDIENTS

PASTRY

- 150 g/5½ oz plain flour, plus extra for dusting
- 85 g/3 oz butter, cut into small pieces, plus extra for greasing
- 35 g/1¼ oz icing sugar, sifted
- finely grated rind of ½ lemon
- ½ egg yolk, beaten
- 1½ tbsp milk

FILLING

- 3 tbsp cornflour
- 300 ml/10 fl oz water
- juice and grated rind of 2 lemons
- 175 g/6 oz caster sugar
- 2 eggs, separated

1 To make the pastry, sift the flour into a bowl. Rub in the butter with your fingertips until the mixture resembles fine breadcrumbs. Mix in the remaining ingredients. Turn out onto a lightly floured work surface and knead briefly. Wrap in clingfilm and chill in the refrigerator for 30 minutes.

2 Preheat the oven to 180°C/350°F/Gas Mark 4. Grease a 20-cm/8-inch round tart tin. Roll out the pastry to a thickness of 5 mm/¼ inch, then use it to line the base and side of the tin. Prick all over with a fork, line with baking paper and fill with baking beans. Bake in the preheated oven for 15 minutes. Remove the pastry case from the oven and take out the paper and beans. Reduce the oven temperature to 150°C/300°F/Gas Mark 2.

3 To make the filling, mix the cornflour with a little of the water to form a paste. Put the remaining water in a saucepan. Stir in the lemon juice, lemon rind and cornflour paste. Bring to the boil, stirring. Cook for 2 minutes. Leave to cool slightly. Stir in 5 tablespoons of the caster sugar and the egg yolks, then pour into the pastry case.

4 Whisk the egg whites in a clean, grease-free bowl until stiff. Gradually whisk in the remaining caster sugar and spread over the pie. Bake for a further 40 minutes. Remove from the oven, cool and serve.

DINNER PARTY WINNER

Lime Pie

SERVES 8

INGREDIENTS

CRUMB CRUST

- 175 g/6 oz digestive or ginger biscuits
- 2 tbsp caster sugar
- ½ tsp ground cinnamon
- 70 g/2½ oz butter, melted, plus extra for greasing

FILLING

- 400 ml/14 fl oz canned condensed milk
- 125 ml/4 fl oz freshly squeezed lime juice
- finely grated rind of 3 limes
- 4 egg yolks
- whipped cream, to serve

1 Preheat the oven to 160°C/325°F/Gas Mark 3. Lightly grease a 23-cm/9-inch round tart tin, about 4 cm/1½ inches deep.

2 To make the crumb crust, put the biscuits, sugar and cinnamon in a food processor and process until fine crumbs form – do not overprocess to a powder. Add the melted butter and process again until moistened.

3 Tip the crumb mixture into the prepared tart tin and press over the base and up the side. Place the tart tin on a baking tray and bake in the preheated oven for 5 minutes.

4 Meanwhile, to make the filling, beat the condensed milk, lime juice, lime rind and egg yolks together in a bowl until well blended.

5 Remove the tart tin from the oven, pour the filling into the crumb crust and spread out to the edges. Return to the oven for a further 15 minutes, or until the filling is set around the edges but still wobbly in the centre.

6 Leave to cool completely on a wire rack, then cover and chill for at least 2 hours. Spread thickly with whipped cream and serve.

Rhubarb Crumble

SERVES 6

INGREDIENTS

• 900 g/2 lb rhubarb
• 115 g/4 oz caster sugar
• grated rind and juice of
  1 orange
• Home-made Vanilla Custard
  (see page 144), to serve

CRUMBLE

• 225 g/8 oz plain flour or
  wholemeal flour
• 115 g/4 oz butter
• 115 g/4 oz soft light
  brown sugar
• 1 tsp ground ginger

1 Preheat the oven to 190°C/375°F/Gas Mark 5.

2 Cut the rhubarb into 2.5-cm/1-inch lengths and place in a 1.7-litre/3-pint ovenproof dish with the sugar and the orange rind and juice.

3 To make the crumble, place the flour in a mixing bowl and rub in the butter until the mixture resembles coarse breadcrumbs. Stir in the sugar and the ginger.

4 Spread the crumble evenly over the fruit and press down lightly using a fork.

5 Place on a baking tray and bake in the centre of the preheated oven for 25–30 minutes, until the crumble is golden brown. Serve warm with Home-made Vanilla Custard.

GRANDMA'S TIP
Use very young shoots of rhubarb as they are the sweetest. A handful of strawberries would be a good addition as they enhance the flavour and colour.

Bread & Butter Pudding

SERVES 4–6

INGREDIENTS

- 85 g/3 oz butter, softened
- 6 slices of thick white bread
- 55 g/2 oz mixed dried fruit, such as sultanas, currants and raisins
- 25 g/1 oz mixed peel
- 3 large eggs
- 300 ml/10 fl oz milk
- 150 ml/5 fl oz double cream
- 55 g/2 oz caster sugar
- whole nutmeg, for grating
- 1 tbsp demerara sugar
- pouring cream, to serve (optional)

1 Preheat the oven to 180°C/350°F/Gas Mark 4.

2 Use a little of the butter to grease a 20 x 25-cm/ 8 x 10-inch baking dish. Butter the slices of bread, cut into quarters and arrange half of the slices overlapping in the prepared baking dish.

3 Scatter half the fruit and mixed peel over the bread, cover with the remaining bread slices, then add the remaining fruit and mixed peel.

4 In a mixing jug, whisk the eggs well and mix in the milk, cream and sugar. Pour over the pudding and leave to stand for 15 minutes to allow the bread to soak up some of the egg mixture. Tuck in most of the fruit as you don't want it to burn in the oven.

5 Grate nutmeg to taste over the top of the pudding, then sprinkle over the demerara sugar.

6 Place the pudding on a baking tray and bake at the top of the preheated oven for 30–40 minutes, until just set and golden brown.

7 Remove from the oven and serve warm with a little cream, if using.

GRANDMA'S TIP
Try using brioche or a lightly fruited loaf instead of white bread. Any mixture of dried fruits can be used. Why not experiment with your favourites?

Baked Rice Pudding

SERVES 4–6

INGREDIENTS

- 1 tbsp melted unsalted butter
- 115 g/4 oz pudding rice
- 55 g/2 oz caster sugar
- 850 ml/1½ pints milk
- ½ tsp vanilla extract
- 40 g/1½ oz unsalted butter, chilled and cut into pieces
- whole nutmeg, for grating
- cream, jam, fresh fruit purée, stewed fruit, honey or ice cream, to serve (optional)

1 Preheat the oven to 150°C/300°F/Gas Mark 2. Grease a 1.2-litre/2-pint baking dish (a gratin dish is good) with the melted butter, place the rice in the dish and sprinkle with the sugar.

2 Heat the milk in a saucepan until almost boiling, then pour over the rice. Add the vanilla extract and stir well to dissolve the sugar.

3 Cut the butter into small pieces and scatter over the surface of the pudding.

4 Grate nutmeg to taste over the top. Place the dish on a baking tray and bake in the centre of the preheated oven for 1½–2 hours until the pudding is well browned on the top. Stir after the first 30 minutes of cooking to disperse the rice. Serve hot, topped with cream, if using.

GRANDMA'S TIP
When measuring honey or syrup, dip the measuring spoon in hot water and dry it first to prevent sticking.

New York Cheesecake

SERVES 10

INGREDIENTS

- 100 g/3½ oz butter, plus extra for greasing
- 150 g/5½ oz digestive biscuits, finely crushed
- 1 tbsp granulated sugar
- 900 g/2 lb cream cheese
- 250 g/9 oz caster sugar
- 2 tbsp plain flour
- 1 tsp vanilla extract
- finely grated zest of 1 orange
- finely grated zest of 1 lemon
- 3 eggs
- 2 egg yolks
- 300 ml/10 fl oz double cream

1 Preheat the oven to 180°C/350°F/Gas Mark 4. Place a small saucepan over a low flame, add the butter and heat until it melts. Remove from the heat, stir in the biscuits and granulated sugar and mix through.

2 Press the biscuit mixture tightly into the base of a 23-cm/9-inch springform cake tin. Place in the preheated oven and bake for 10 minutes. Remove from the oven and leave to cool on a wire rack.

3 Increase the oven temperature to 200°C/400°F/Gas Mark 6. Use an electric mixer to beat the cheese until creamy, then gradually add the caster sugar and flour and beat until smooth. Increase the speed and beat in the vanilla extract, orange zest and lemon zest, then beat in the eggs and egg yolks one at a time. Finally, beat in the cream. Scrape any excess from the sides and paddles of the beater into the mixture. It should be light and fluffy – beat on a faster setting if you need to.

4 Grease the side of the cake tin and pour in the filling. Smooth the top, transfer to the oven and bake for 15 minutes, then reduce the temperature to 110°C/225°F/Gas Mark ¼ and bake for a further 30 minutes. Turn off the oven and leave the cheesecake in it for 2 hours to cool and set. Cover and chill in the refrigerator overnight.

5 Slide a knife around the edge of the cake then unfasten the tin, cut the cheesecake into slices and serve.

GRANDMA'S GUILTY PLEASURE

Sticky Toffee Pudding

SERVES 4

INGREDIENTS

PUDDING

- 75 g/2¾ oz sultanas
- 150 g/5½ oz stoned dates, chopped
- 1 tsp bicarbonate of soda
- 2 tbsp butter, plus extra for greasing
- 200 g/7 oz soft light brown sugar
- 2 eggs
- 200 g/7 oz self-raising flour, sifted

STICKY TOFFEE SAUCE

- 2 tbsp butter
- 175 ml/6 fl oz double cream
- 200 g/7 oz soft light brown sugar
- zested rind of 1 orange, to decorate
- freshly whipped cream, to serve (optional)

1 To make the pudding, put the sultanas, dates and bicarbonate of soda into a heatproof bowl. Cover with boiling water and leave to soak.

2 Preheat the oven to 180°C/350°F/Gas Mark 4. Grease a round cake tin, 20 cm/8 inches in diameter.

3 Put the butter in a separate bowl, add the sugar and mix well. Beat in the eggs then fold in the flour. Drain the soaked fruit, add to the bowl and mix. Spoon the mixture evenly into the prepared cake tin.

4 Transfer to the preheated oven and bake for 35–40 minutes. The pudding is cooked when a skewer inserted into the centre comes out clean.

5 About 5 minutes before the end of the cooking time, make the sauce. Melt the butter in a saucepan over a medium heat. Stir in the cream and sugar and bring to the boil, stirring constantly. Reduce the heat and simmer for 5 minutes.

6 Turn out the pudding onto a serving plate and pour over the sauce. Decorate with zested orange rind and serve with whipped cream, if using.

GRANDMA'S TIP
You can make this wicked pudding in individual pudding basins so that everyone has their own portion. Cook for 20–25 minutes and then turn out onto serving plates.

Chocolate Pudding

SERVES 4–6

INGREDIENTS

- 100 g/3½ oz sugar
- 4 tbsp cocoa powder
- 2 tbsp cornflour
- pinch of salt
- 350 ml/12 fl oz milk
- 1 egg, beaten
- 55 g/2 oz butter
- ½ tsp vanilla extract
- double cream,
  to serve

1 Put the sugar, cocoa powder, cornflour and salt into a heatproof bowl, stir and set aside.

2 Pour the milk into a saucepan and heat over a medium heat until just simmering. Do not bring to the boil.

3 Keeping the pan over a medium heat, spoon a little of the simmering milk into the sugar mixture and blend, then stir this mixture into the milk in the pan. Beat in the egg and half the butter and reduce the heat to low.

4 Simmer for 5–8 minutes, stirring frequently, until the mixture thickens. Remove from the heat and add the vanilla extract and the remaining butter, stirring until the butter melts and is absorbed.

5 The pudding can be served hot or chilled, with cream for pouring over. If chilling the pudding, spoon it into a serving bowl and leave to cool completely, then press clingfilm onto the surface to prevent a skin forming and chill in the refrigerator until required.

Chocolate Fudge

MAKES 32 PIECES

INGREDIENTS

- 2 tbsp cocoa powder
- 300 ml/10 fl oz milk mixture
- 125 g/4½ oz plain chocolate, at least 85 per cent cocoa solids, finely chopped
- 800 g/1 lb 12 oz caster sugar
- 125 g/4½ oz butter, chopped, plus extra for greasing
- pinch of salt
- 1½ tsp vanilla extract
- 175 g/6 oz pecan nuts, walnuts or toasted hazelnuts, or a mixture of nuts, chopped

1 Put the cocoa powder into a small bowl, add 2 tablespoons of the milk and stir until blended. Pour the remaining milk into a large, heavy-based saucepan, then add the cocoa mixture and chocolate and simmer over a medium–high heat, stirring, until the chocolate melts. Add the sugar, butter and salt, reduce the heat to low and stir until the butter is melted, the sugar is dissolved and you can't feel any of the grains when you rub a spoon against the side of the pan.

2 Increase the heat and bring the milk mixture to the boil. Cover the pan and boil for 2 minutes, then uncover and carefully clip a sugar thermometer to the side. Continue boiling, without stirring, until the temperature reaches 115°C/239°F, or until a small amount of the mixture forms a soft ball when dropped in cold water.

3 Meanwhile, line a 20-cm/8-inch square cake tin with foil, grease the foil, then set aside.

4 Remove the pan from the heat, stir in the vanilla extract and beat the fudge until it thickens. Stir in the nuts.

5 Pour the fudge mixture into the prepared tin and use a wet spatula to smooth the surface. Set aside and leave to stand for at least 2 hours to become firm. Lift the fudge out of the tin, then peel off the foil. Cut the fudge into eight 2.5-cm/1-inch strips, then cut each strip into four pieces. Store the fudge for up to one week in an airtight container.

Pecan Pie

SERVES 8

INGREDIENTS

PASTRY

- 200 g/7 oz plain flour, plus extra for dusting
- 115 g/4 oz unsalted butter
- 2 tbsp caster sugar
- a little cold water

FILLING

- 70 g/2½ oz unsalted butter
- 100 g/3½ oz light muscovado sugar
- 140 g/5 oz golden syrup
- 2 large eggs, beaten
- 1 tsp vanilla extract
- 115 g/4 oz pecan nuts

1 To make the pastry, place the flour in a bowl and rub in the butter with your fingertips until it resembles fine breadcrumbs. Stir in the sugar and add enough cold water to mix to a firm dough. Wrap in clingfilm and chill for 15 minutes, until firm enough to roll out.

2 Preheat the oven to 200°C/400°F/Gas Mark 6. Roll out the pastry on a lightly floured surface and use to line a 23-cm/9-inch loose-based round tart tin. Prick the base with a fork. Chill for 15 minutes.

3 Place the tart tin on a baking tray and line with a sheet of baking paper and baking beans. Bake blind in the preheated oven for 10 minutes. Remove the baking beans and paper and bake for a further 5 minutes. Reduce the oven temperature to 180°C/350°F/Gas Mark 4.

4 To make the filling, place the butter, sugar and golden syrup in a saucepan and heat gently until melted. Remove from the heat and quickly beat in the eggs and vanilla extract.

5 Roughly chop the nuts and stir into the mixture. Pour into the pastry case and bake for 35–40 minutes, until the filling is just set. Serve warm or cold.

GRANDMA'S TIP
Add 2 tablespoons of dark rum to the filling just before removing it from the heat. This will balance the sweetness and bring out the rich flavours.

Pumpkin Pie

SERVES 6
INGREDIENTS

- 1.8 kg/4 lb sweet pumpkin, halved and deseeded, stem and stringy bits removed
- 140 g/5 oz plain flour, plus extra for dusting
- ¼ tsp baking powder
- 1½ tsp ground cinnamon
- ¾ tsp ground nutmeg
- ¾ tsp ground cloves
- 1 tsp salt
- 50 g/1¾ oz caster sugar
- 55 g/2 oz cold unsalted butter, diced, plus extra for greasing
- 3 eggs
- 400 ml/14 fl oz canned condensed milk
- ½ tsp vanilla extract
- 1 tbsp demerara sugar

STREUSEL TOPPING
- 2 tbsp plain flour
- 4 tbsp demerara sugar
- 1 tsp ground cinnamon
- 2 tbsp cold unsalted butter, diced
- 75 g/2¾ oz pecan nuts, chopped
- 75 g/2¾ oz walnuts, chopped

1 Preheat the oven to 190°C/375°F/Gas Mark 5. Put the pumpkin halves, face down, in a shallow baking tin and cover with foil. Bake in the preheated oven for 1½ hours, then leave to cool. Scoop out the flesh and purée in a food processor. Drain off any excess liquid. Cover and chill.

2 Grease a 23-cm/9-inch round tart tin. Sift the flour and baking powder into a large bowl. Stir in ½ teaspoon of the cinnamon, ¼ teaspoon of the nutmeg, ¼ teaspoon of the cloves, ½ teaspoon of the salt and all the caster sugar.

3 Rub in the butter with your fingertips until the mixture resembles fine breadcrumbs, then make a well in the centre. Lightly beat 1 of the eggs and pour it into the well. Mix together with a wooden spoon, then shape the dough into a ball. Turn out the dough onto a lightly floured work surface, roll out and use to line the prepared tin. Trim the edges, then cover and chill for 30 minutes.

4 Preheat the oven to 220°C/425°F/Gas Mark 7. Put the pumpkin purée in a large bowl, then stir in the condensed milk and the remaining eggs. Add the remaining spices and salt, then stir in the vanilla extract and demerara sugar. Pour into the pastry case and bake in the preheated oven for 15 minutes.

5 Meanwhile, make the streusel topping. Mix the flour, sugar and cinnamon together in a bowl, rub in the butter, then stir in the nuts. Remove the pie from the oven and reduce the oven temperature to 180°C/350°F/Gas Mark 4. Sprinkle over the topping, then return to the oven and bake for a further 35 minutes.

IMPRESS THE FAMILY

Latticed Cherry Pie

SERVES 8

INGREDIENTS

PASTRY
- 140 g/5 oz plain flour, plus extra for dusting
- ¼ tsp baking powder
- ½ tsp mixed spice
- ½ tsp salt
- 50 g/1¾ oz caster sugar
- 55 g/2 oz unsalted butter, chilled and diced, plus extra for greasing
- 1 egg, beaten, plus extra for glazing
- water, for sealing

FILLING
- 900 g/2 lb stoned fresh cherries, or canned cherries, drained
- 150 g/5½ oz caster sugar
- ½ tsp almond extract
- 2 tsp cherry brandy
- 1/4 tsp mixed spice
- 2 tbsp cornflour
- 2 tbsp water
- 25 g/1 oz unsalted butter, melted

1 To make the pastry, sift the flour with the baking powder into a large bowl. Stir in the mixed spice, salt and sugar. Rub the butter until the mixture resembles fine breadcrumbs, make a well in the centre, pour in the egg and mix into a dough. Cut the dough in half, and use your hands to roll each half into a ball. Wrap and chill for 30 minutes.

2 Preheat the oven to 220°C/425°F/Gas Mark 7. Grease a 23-cm/9-inch round pie dish. Roll out the doughs into two rounds, each 30 cm/12 inches in diameter. Use one to line the pie dish.

3 To make the filling, put half the cherries and all the sugar in a saucepan. Bring to a simmer and stir in the almond extract, brandy and mixed spice. In a bowl, mix the cornflour and water into a paste. Stir the paste into the saucepan, then boil until the mixture thickens. Stir in the remaining cherries, pour into the pastry case, then dot with butter.

4 Cut the remaining pastry into strips 1 cm/½ inch wide. Lay the strips over the filling, crossing to form a lattice. Trim and seal the edges with water. Use your fingers to crimp around the rim, then glaze the top with the beaten egg. Cover with kitchen foil, then bake for 30 minutes in the preheated oven.

5 Remove from the oven, discard the foil, then bake for a further 15 minutes, or until golden. Serve warm.

GRANDMA'S TIP
Chilling the pastry after making it enables the dough to relax and so minimizes the chances of it shrinking during cooking.

Baked Spicy Pudding

SERVES 4–6

INGREDIENTS

- 2 tbsp raisins or sultanas
- 5 tbsp polenta
- 350 ml/12 fl oz milk
- 4 tbsp treacle
- 2 tbsp soft dark
  brown sugar
- ½ tsp salt
- 30 g/1 oz butter, diced,
  plus extra for greasing
- 2 tsp ground ginger
- ¼ tsp cinnamon
- ¼ tsp ground nutmeg
- 2 eggs, beaten
- vanilla ice cream or maple
  syrup, to serve

1 Preheat the oven to 150°C/300°F/ Gas Mark 2. Generously grease a 900-ml/1½-pint ovenproof serving dish and set aside. Put the raisins in a sieve with 1 tablespoon of the polenta and toss well together. Shake off the excess polenta and set aside.

2 Put the milk and treacle into a saucepan over a medium–high heat and stir until the treacle is dissolved. Add the sugar and salt and continue stirring until the sugar is dissolved. Sprinkle over the remaining polenta and bring to the boil, stirring constantly. Reduce the heat and simmer for 3–5 minutes, until the mixture is thickened.

3 Remove the pan from the heat, add the butter, ginger, cinnamon and nutmeg and stir until the butter is melted. Add the eggs and beat until they are incorporated, then stir in the raisins. Pour the mixture into the prepared dish.

4 Put the dish in a small roasting tin and pour in enough boiling water to come halfway up the side of the dish. Put the dish in the preheated oven and bake, uncovered, for 1¾–2 hours, until the pudding is set and a wooden skewer inserted in the centre comes out clean.

5 Serve immediately, straight from the dish, with a dollop of ice cream on top.

Apple Turnovers

MAKES 8 TURNOVERS
INGREDIENTS

- 250 g/9 oz ready-made puff pastry, thawed, if frozen
- milk, for glazing

FILLING

- 450 g/1 lb cooking apples, peeled, cored and chopped
- grated rind of 1 lemon (optional)
- pinch of ground cloves (optional)
- 3 tbsp sugar

ORANGE SUGAR

- 1 tbsp sugar, for sprinkling
- finely grated rind of 1 orange

ORANGE CREAM

- 250 ml/9 fl oz double cream
- grated rind of 1 orange and juice of ½ orange
- icing sugar, to taste

1 Prepare the filling before rolling out the pastry. Mix together the apples, lemon rind and ground cloves, if using, but do not add the sugar until the last minute because this will cause the juice to seep out of the apples. For the orange sugar, mix together the sugar and orange rind.

2 Preheat the oven to 220°C/425°F/Gas Mark 7. Roll out the pastry on a floured work surface into a 60 × 30-cm/24 × 12-inch rectangle. Cut the pastry in half lengthways, then across into four to make eight 15-cm/6-inch squares. (You can do this in two batches, rolling half of the pastry out into a 30-cm/12-inch square and cutting it into quarters, if preferred.)

3 Mix the sugar into the apple filling. Brush each square lightly with milk and place a little of the apple filling in the centre. Fold over one corner diagonally to meet the opposite one, making a triangular turnover, and press the edges together very firmly. Place on a non-stick baking sheet. Repeat with the remaining squares.

4 Brush the turnovers with milk and sprinkle with a little of the orange sugar. Bake for 15–20 minutes, until puffed and well browned. Cool the turnovers on a wire rack.

5 For the orange cream, whip the cream, orange rind and orange juice together until thick. Add a little sugar to taste and whip again until the cream just holds soft peaks. Serve the turnovers warm, with dollops of orange cream.

> **GRANDMA'S TIP**
> For something extra warming, try adding some cinnamon, or replace the lemon rind with orange rind and a teaspoon of marmalade.

Apple Fritters

MAKES 12 FRITTERS
INGREDIENTS

- 300 g/10½ oz eating apples, such as Granny Smith, peeled, cored and diced
- 1 tsp lemon juice
- 2 eggs, separated
- 150 ml/5 fl oz milk
- 15 g/½ oz butter, melted
- 70 g/2½ oz plain white flour
- 70 g/2½ oz plain wholemeal flour
- 2 tbsp sugar
- ¼ tsp salt
- sunflower oil, for deep-frying and greasing

CINNAMON GLAZE
- 55 g/2 oz icing sugar
- ½ tsp ground cinnamon
- 1 tbsp milk, plus extra, if needed

1 To make the cinnamon glaze, sift the sugar and cinnamon into a small bowl and make a well in the centre. Slowly stir in the milk until smooth, then set aside.

2 Put the apples in a small bowl, add the lemon juice, toss and set aside. Beat the egg whites in a separate bowl until stiff peaks form, then set aside.

3 Heat enough oil for deep-frying in a deep-fat fryer or heavy-based saucepan until it reaches 180°C/350°F, or until a cube of bread browns in 30 seconds.

4 Meanwhile, put the egg yolks and milk into a large bowl and beat together, then stir in the butter. Sift in the white flour, wholemeal flour, sugar and salt, tipping in any bran left in the sieve, then

stir the dry ingredients into the wet ingredients until just combined. Stir in the apples and their juices, then fold in the egg whites.

5 Lightly grease a spoon and use it to drop batter into the hot oil, without overcrowding the pan. Fry the fritters for 2–3 minutes, turning once, until golden brown on both sides. Transfer to kitchen paper to drain, then transfer to a wire rack. Repeat this process until all the batter is used.

6 Stir the glaze and add a little extra milk, if necessary, so that it flows freely from the tip of a spoon. Drizzle the glaze over the fritters and leave to stand for 3–5 minutes to firm up. Serve immediately.

GRANDMA'S TIP
If not serving the fritters right away, sift over some icing sugar, cinnamon and a pinch of nutmeg, then leave to cool. These are best eaten on the day they are made, however.

Banana Splits

SERVES 4

INGREDIENTS

- 4 bananas
- 6 tbsp chopped mixed nuts,
  to serve

VANILLA ICE CREAM

- 300 ml/10 fl oz milk
- 1 tsp vanilla extract
- 3 egg yolks
- 100 g/3½ oz caster sugar
- 300 ml/10 fl oz double
  cream, whipped

CHOCOLATE RUM SAUCE

- 125 g/4½ oz plain chocolate,
  broken into small pieces
- 2½ tbsp butter
- 6 tbsp water
- 1 tbsp rum

1 To make the vanilla ice cream, heat the milk and vanilla extract in a saucepan over a medium heat until almost boiling. Beat the egg yolks and sugar together in a bowl. Remove the milk from the heat and stir a little into the egg mixture. Transfer the mixture to the pan and stir over a low heat until thickened. Do not allow to boil. Remove from the heat.

2 Leave to cool for about 30 minutes, fold in the cream, cover with clingfilm and chill in the refrigerator for 1 hour. Transfer to an ice-cream maker and process for 15 minutes.

3 Alternatively, transfer into a freezerproof container and freeze for 1 hour, then place in a bowl and beat to break up the ice crystals. Return to the container and freeze for 30 minutes. Repeat twice more, freezing for 30 minutes and whisking each time.

4 To make the chocolate rum sauce, melt the chocolate and butter with the water in a saucepan, stirring constantly. Remove from the heat and stir in the rum. Peel the bananas, slice lengthways and arrange on four serving dishes. Top with ice cream and nuts and serve with the sauce.

GRANDMA'S TIP
For a quick and easy pudding, use shop-bought ice cream. If you're serving the banana splits to children, omit the rum from the chocolate sauce.

Created with
love by
....

Baked with love
by
....

TRY THESE TASTY
....
DATE MADE
....
INGREDIENTS
....

Baked with
love by
....

Created with love by
....

TRY THESE TASTY
....
DATE MADE
....
INGREDIENTS
....
....

Baked with
love by
....

Created with love
by
....

Baked with love
by
....

TRY THESE TASTY
....
DATE MADE
....
INGREDIENTS
....
....

Baked with
love by
....

Created with love by
....

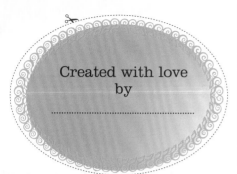

Created with love by

Baked with love by

Created with love by

Baked with love by

Created with love by

Baked with love by

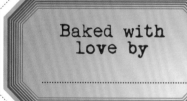

Baked with love by

TRY THESE TASTY

DATE MADE

INGREDIENTS

Created with love by

TRY THESE TASTY

DATE MADE

INGREDIENTS

Baked with love by

TRY THESE TASTY

DATE MADE

INGREDIENTS